How Can I
PRAY
For You

---✧---

The Revelation
That Changed Everything

Caron Carroll

Endorsements

This book belongs in every Christian's library who carries the desire to make Heaven crowded. With warmth, clarity, and compassion, Caron Carroll takes the Great Commission and makes it doable in today's world. Through relatable examples and practical steps, she shows us how simple acts of love and kindness can open doors for the gospel.

How Can I Pray for You? Is more than a book, it's a powerful tool that equips anyone with a heart for God to reach the hurting, bring hope, and share Christ's love in everyday moments. This is a resource every church could place in the hands of individuals eager to love well and share the gospel with those who need it most. Well Done!

~Missy Maxwell Worton
Award-Winning Author of *Don't Mess With this Mama*
CEO & Founder Warrior Writer's Community and
Light Warrior Publishing

Caron is on a mission to populate Heaven. She has a genuine love for people and a sincere passion for seeing lives transformed by Jesus.

This inspiring book is a heartfelt guide on how to pray for people and share the gospel. I especially appreciate her clear and uncomplicated approach to sharing the Good News.

Gifted in evangelism and driven by a deep compassion for others, she inspires readers to share the Good News with the same warmth and boldness she lives out daily. Her words will encourage you to step boldly into evangelism, equipping you with simple, practical ways to share your faith

Through relatable examples from her own journey, Caron makes evangelism approachable for anyone, whether you're just starting out or have been serving the Lord for years but still desire to grow in this area. We're all called to share the gospel.

This book will leave you both encouraged and equipped to pray for others and share your faith with confidence.

~Terri Gilbert
Entrepreneur, Author & Speaker

Dedications

To my Heavenly Father. You surprised me with the invitation to write. I had no idea what would come of it—only that you clearly said, "Just write."

Thank you for revealing something so magnificent—something I would have missed had I not come searching for purpose and identity. Through this journey, You healed my heart, patiently teaching me through every page.

Every chain that held me back is now broken because You showed me who I am in You. What I thought was a story of healing turned out to be Yours all along—a story meant to reveal who You are.

Gone are the days of not knowing You. My heart now flows with joy, peace, and gratitude. I love You so much!

To my earthly father, Charles (Chuck) Cunning, who left this world far too soon.

Dad, there isn't a day that goes by that I don't wish you were here. I would have loved to share my latest writings, just as you shared yours with me. But I know you are part of that cloud of witnesses cheering me on from heaven. Before I ever began writing, I wondered how you turned life into words—now I know! I can't wait to hear you say, "You did it! Good job!"

I miss you in every way a daughter could miss her dad.

I love you so much, Dad!

Table of Contents

Forewords

Prayer is one of the most intimate and powerful gifts we can offer another person. In my journey of faith, I've come to realize that the question "How can I pray for you?" is more than just kind words—it's an invitation into someone's heart, a bridge to their burdens, and a sacred moment of partnership with God. This book was born out of that simple question, asked countless times in coffee shops, hospital rooms, church altars, on the street, in the marketplace, and in everyday conversations. Inside these pages, you'll find not just encouragement but practical wisdom and Spirit-led insight to help you pray with compassion, clarity, and boldness. You'll walk the journey of Caron's path into a ministry which has touched countless lives. Whether you're stepping into prayer ministry for the first time, looking to go deeper, or to just encouraged by a walk of faith, it is my prayer Caron's story ignites a fire in your heart—to listen well, love deeply, and pray faithfully for those God places in your path.

~Bishop Shawn Baker, President of PSB MINISTRIES, Senior Pastor, New Life Church

Caron Caroll writes from a place of honesty, transparency, and real-life experience. She does not merely hear the Word of God—she lives it. Her journey and testimony flow through these pages, reminding us that the call to follow Christ is not reserved for the few who appear "qualified" but for every believer who dares to say yes to God.

Her words challenge us to walk boldly and courageously, knowing that each of us has a divine assignment. We are all commissioned to share the gospel, to reach the lost, and to make disciples. In Caron's stories, you will find both encouragement and conviction—a reminder that the Great Commission is not optional, but essential.

In these last days, when the harvest is truly plentiful, her writings urge us to be vigilant and unwavering, just as Jesus was, in seeking and saving the lost. May every page inspire you to rise up, to trust the power of the Holy Spirit, and to step into the calling God has placed on your life.

This is more than a book—it is a charge to the Body of Christ.

~**Cherie Anderson**, Evangelist and Author of *The Gospel Made Simple*

Author's Note to the Reader

Dear Reader:

Did you know God wrote a book about you? Before the world was created, before you took your first breath, before you were ever given a name, God had already written a story—yours.

The day I first heard Psalm 139:16 NLT, something in me shifted.

"You saw me before I was born. Every day of my life was recorded in your book. Every moment was laid out before a single day had passed."

I remember sitting in awe after reading that Scripture, wondering... *What did You write about me, God? What dreams? What assignments? What kind of love would move You to plan my days before I ever took my first breath?*

It was more than just a beautiful verse—it was personal.

That verse pierced through the clamor of shame, rejection, doubt, and fear. It told me I had purpose that was authored by the Creator Himself. And if God wrote a book about me, then I didn't want to settle for a single chapter less than He intended. I wanted to live every page of it, and still do, because I know His plans are good and they won't hurt me.

I believe the same is true for you.

You are not here by chance. Long before you were born, God dreamed of you. He handcrafted your personality, your purpose, and your journey. He saw every moment of your life—and He still chose to write your story with love. That means your life has meaning. It has direction. It has value beyond what you've believed, felt, or even experienced.

My prayer is that as you read this book, you will begin to see yourself the way God sees you: fully known, deeply loved, and divinely purposed. I hope you'll dare to ask Him, "Lord, show me what You wrote about me." And when He begins to reveal it, I pray you'll have the courage to walk in it.

You were created for more—and heaven has it recorded in your book.

With love and expectancy,

Caron Carroll

Chapter One
Created for More

"This is what the Lord says:
'Stop at the crossroads and look around.
Ask for the old, godly way, and walk in it.
Travel its path, and you will find rest for your souls.'"
Jeremiah 6:16 NLT

The Quiet Ache

Not that I felt empty exactly, but the question kept cycling through my mind: *Is there more?*

Have you ever wondered about that?

I was deeply loved, happily married to Joey, and closely connected to my children, grandchildren, and friends. Yet, something inside me stirred—a quiet ache, a sense that something was missing. A longing. Not a longing for more stuff or more success—it wasn't even about a new career.

It was deeper. A God-given purpose I hadn't yet tapped into.

At fifty years old, surrounded by good things and content in many ways, I still wasn't fully content. Do you know what I mean?

Life was full, but my soul was still thirsty.

A Heart Awakening

That's when I realized I had spent half a century on this earth, yet I didn't truly know the One who created and loved me. And with that, profound questions began to stir in my heart:

1. What kind of legacy am I going to leave behind?
2. Do I want the next fifty years to resemble the last fifty?
3. What should those years look like?
4. Did God create me for more than I had been living?
5. What if I died and didn't know the answers to those questions?

But this question stopped me in my tracks:

"Who is God to me?"

I realized I hadn't considered God's wisdom or counsel in most of my life's decisions up to that point, but I sure welcomed His rescues. Though I had been in and out of church my whole life, I now recognized a void. It was subtle, quiet—almost like depression creeping in again. I felt guilty for feeling this way, especially since my marriage was so good—how could I need anything else?

Simultaneously, I was worn out from my high-paced, demanding job in the medical field. Perfection felt like a requirement, creating a "walking on eggshells" kind of environment for me. My soul craved something different: peace. But I felt stuck, burned out, and bound to a "fake it till you make it" kind of life until retirement.

The Vision

One ordinary day, in my living room, I had a strange experience. I had a vision in my mind's eye. I stood alone at a crossroads in the middle of a dry, barren desert. No trees. No animals. No mirage. Just me.

I dismissed it at first, but the image kept returning. Scenes from my life—memories, hurts, heartbreak, motherhood, blessings—and wondered: *Where is my path leading? Which way would I go?*

Although the last fifty years were filled with countless blessings, they were also marked by pain and confusion stemming from a long season of brokenness that began years ago.

Looking Back—The Shattered Season

My first marriage, to my children's dad, ended in divorce. When we married, I had no clear vision for my life—just a desire to be a good wife and mother, which felt like my highest calling. Having a career and a nice home I could decorate was a close second on my list of priorities.

But deep down, I was entangled in strongholds I didn't yet understand—personal battles wrapped around our marriage like a python slowly squeezing life from both of us. It was hard to describe.

As if life weren't hard enough, a sudden call came that shattered my world completely.

"Daddo's dead! Your dad is dead!"

Breathing was painful as my knees hit the floor. My tears soaked into the carpet as I cried out, unable to process the news. He was only sixty-six years old and had just retired—gone forever. That news was painfully shocking and mentally devastating for me and my family.

Gone was my anchor. My rock. The man my kids lovingly called "Daddo." No last "I love you." No more chances to have a hug or to ask, "Dad, what do you think about this or that?" My heart broke wide open.

Grieving my dad amidst a crumbling marriage was agonizing. I was feeling the excruciating pain of lost dreams to have a strong, healthy, loving marriage and family. But it seemed the harder I fought, the tighter the python's grip tightened.

When the divorce happened, I was convinced I could not be in God's will, as if I knew God was done with a sinner such as I was. I believed divorce was the one sin that would never be forgiven, so why try to be good now? What would be the point?

But the losses kept coming. One by one, everything I cherished slipped away. In six years, I lost nearly everything that defined me:

- My dad
- My marriage of 18 years
- My home to bankruptcy
- My mom
- My sense of identity as my children grew up and moved on.

I felt like an orphan. Like Job, who lost everything, I felt lost in a life of unpredictability. Drenched in grief, shame, rejection, and fear—anxiety was crushing me. Then, there was alcohol—my counterfeit comfort—something I leaned into even more during this season of loss.

An Unlikely Love

Trying to hold myself together, I told myself I could be content alone, but the truth was—I didn't want to be. Considering my past experiences, I was highly suspicious of any man who offered me a relationship.

That's when Joey came into my life.

I tried to push him away, *"Don't love me! Just go away!"* My life was too messy and complicated. I couldn't risk the possibility of one more broken relationship attaching itself to me. I didn't trust myself to make a decent decision, so how could I trust another person?

But Joey loved me anyway. Through all of my doubts. Through my brokenness, his steady and reassuring love softened my heart. I felt seen and for the first time in my life, I believed I could be loved—just as I am.

When I let go of apprehensions, he swept me off my feet! Unlike any love I had ever encountered, I wondered why I would deserve such a gift. I felt like a beloved princess who had met her prince charming, not that I deserved it, but because he chose to shower me with undeniable love and honor.

We didn't date long before getting engaged. Our wedding day was one of the most beautiful days of my life! It was a few years after my heart had softened under Joey's tender love, that the longing for more began. Not in *our* relationship—Joey was everything I had hoped for—but inside of me, there was a subtle sense that something was missing.

Back to the Crossroads

I began to understand that the desert crossroads that I saw in my vision were showing me my past, which became the stepping stones that awakened my soul yearning to know the One who made me. A deep spiritual ache to know my Heavenly Father intimately had developed in the desert. An invitation my awakening heart recognized.

The desert was God's place to reveal the condition of my heart, so He could heal it. With baby steps, I began to believe that God had placed a purpose within me.

The First Step

My journey to discover God's plan for me started by waking up ten minutes earlier every day to pray beside my bed. Sometimes, I didn't even know what to say, but a song by the Christian band Third Day became my prayer, asking God to "give me a revelation and show me what to do." Trying to find my way to God, I played it every day on repeat, getting ready for work. I was beginning to feel spiritually strengthened. Then, out of the blue, I was wrongly accused at work. No warning. No chance to speak. I was shut down.

I cried so hard that it was tough to catch my breath or maintain any dignity at that point–BUT GOD!

When I got home, I was an emotional basket case. So much so, that I struggled telling Joey the whole story. When I finally got it all out, he looked at me with understanding and said, "You should quit."

He didn't have to tell me twice! No one ever supported me like that in my life. I was shocked and overjoyed!

I drove to work the next day with a whole new level of confidence. I felt so loved and supported! On the last day of my two-week notice in April 2019, I updated my Facebook status to read, **"Today is the first day of the rest of my life."**

I didn't know exactly what was next. But I knew this: I didn't want to keep walking without God. That quiet ache and longing for *more*, was for Him all along.

And this time, I was ready to follow.

Chapter Two
The Revelation

"Ask me and I will tell you remarkable secrets you do not know about things to come."
(Jeremiah 33:3 NLT)

The Coastal Pull

For most of my life, the Emerald Coast in Florida—also known as the Miracle Strip—had been my go-to getaway. I had visited those translucent, blue-green waters since I was three years old. I found something captivating about the warm, salty air, the sun on my skin, the powdery, white sand, and the fresh shrimp.

As I was asking God about *the more,* the beach felt like it was calling Joey and me. It constantly stirred something in us, but in this season of seeking God, it became a real possibility.

We almost moved because of a business opportunity for Joey, but that fell through. We were disappointed, but it was hard to let go the dream once the thought had taken root. We began to imagine what life would be like living in a coastal town. And in time, God made a way. It felt a little bit like "Jehovah Sneaky" (a playful term for God's surprising way of working behind the scenes) because I thought I was chasing the beach…but God was chasing my heart, directly responding to my questions.

A Dream Within a Dream

I slowly began to see the coast for what it truly was: a God-given dream planted within me before I even knew it, before I knew how to dream with God. He was drawing me here, not just for the beach but for a greater purpose.

Though we were excited, embracing it was challenging because it meant leaving my children and grandchildren, which didn't make sense. But because it was God, there was a peace—unlike any peace I'd ever known. There was an undeniable green light in my spirit, urging me to move forward. Looking back, it was clearly God's hand—a divine setup—a search for identity.

On August 25, 2019, at 5:53 p.m., Joey and I drove across the bay, bringing everything we owned. My husband had diligently and strategically orchestrated all our plans—but it was God that supernaturally opened every door for this move. I watched the bright yellow Penske truck in my rear-view mirror as Joey followed close behind me. With one hand on the wheel, I grabbed my phone to capture the moment with a quick video. I heard the lyrics playing on the radio, "Give me the beat, boys, and free my soul."

It was surreal. I felt free. For once, I believed I was doing what was right in God's eyes, and I wasn't worried about what others thought. I was stepping into a dream I didn't fully understand, yet I deeply sensed. I had only a small glimpse of the vision, but God is always up to so much more than I could ever imagine.

He was shifting me into a new season in which my identity would no longer be defined by what I did but by who I was in Him.

The Driveway Revelation

We had only been in our new home a short time when I stood in the driveway, in awe of God, trusting and *believing* Him. At fifty-two, the revelation hit me—I had been in a forty-year wilderness.

Wait, what?! I did the math—it had been 40 years since I asked Jesus into my heart. But what does that even mean?

What is a 40-Year Wilderness?

I had heard about the wilderness in the Bible but knew very little about that story. *Who were the children of Israel, and what were they doing in the wilderness?* The wandering, the manna, the complaining, the Promised Land? It's like it was more than a story in the Bible—it was *my* story. The disobedience, distance from God, the idols, not because He had left me, but because I moved from God.

Awakened Faith

At age twelve, I asked Jesus to save me, but I was not sure from what. I never made Him Lord and developed a relationship. Hoping for the heavenly benefit, I believed *in* Him and believed He died and rose from the dead.

I went to church and got "God bumps" on certain songs. I even prayed when I needed Him, but I didn't *know* Him. I called myself a believer, but deep down, I was anything but. I was what I now call an *unbelieving believer*—I was believing lies about myself, failing to grasp who God was to me.

In less than a year after saying a prayer and being baptized, my heart had drifted toward the ways of the world—searching for fulfillment in things that left me feeling empty. My faith was lukewarm, at best. Throughout my life, I let the wrong things define what only God could fulfill—because, deep down, I didn't know how to let God love me.

I began connecting the dots when I had that revelation on the driveway. The wilderness was about my heart. I had never said yes to Jesus. My lack of surrender kept me circling the same mountains of doubt, struggling with disobedience, and not *knowing* Him for decades.

That's when something shifted—an awakened faith I didn't expect. With exuberant praise, I proclaimed, "I believe You now! I want to know You and Your word and stand on it!"

"But seek first the kingdom of God and His righteousness, and all these things shall be added to you."
(Matthew 6:33 NKJV)

A Tangible Encounter

A hunger and thirst stirred in me, not just to learn about the Israelites' journey, but my own. God gave me little bits of my story and how it reflected a new mission. My 40-year journey through the wilderness was becoming foundational to my calling.

This revelation transformed me when I realized I had moved spiritually from a dry and barren land into one rich with peace, joy, rest, intimacy with God, and settled assurance of His love. God was leading me into His Promised Land.

Revelation doesn't whisper—it awakens.

The physical process of moving sparked a spiritual encounter that began to change my mindset. I felt such peace and a deep connection to my Heavenly Father there, as if I could hear Him say, "I have given you the desires of your heart, which is Me!"

I fell in love with the Lord as the awe of His presence washed over me. All my senses were heightened; I encountered a tangible God. For months afterward, I often smelled a floral fragrance around me, connecting me to heaven. Suddenly, I was hit with an understanding of the Scripture, "Taste and see that the Lord is good" (Psalms 34:8 NIV). And indeed, He was good and still is! This was the beginning of my deeper walk with God.

Identity and Intimacy

When I opened my heart and allowed God to love me, everything changed. For the first time, I felt incredibly loved and was able to love Him back. My identity as His daughter started to come into focus. My perspective on life shifted. I had never known anything like this.

> **"This means that anyone who belongs to Christ
> has become a new person.
> The old life is gone; a new life has begun!"
> (2 Corinthians 5:17 NLT)**

The Call to Share

The beach would become a mission field. The peace I used to find worshipping the *sun* has been replaced by something far greater—worshipping the *Son* on these very shores. A fire ignited in me to share the life-changing news I had received. I felt an urgency. *Everyone needs to know what I have found!*

But one question lingered, "How?"

Have you ever asked yourself the same question?

If you're anything like me, you long to see God move in your community. However, when it comes to sharing your faith, maybe you feel unsure, hesitant, or even afraid. What do you say? Where do you start?

It's no accident you're holding this book. You were created for such a time as this. Maybe God is stirring something in your heart, too! Could it be that He's calling you to pray for your community?

The Shores of Grace

That's why I wrote this book—to share my journey of stepping out in faith, even when it was uncomfortable, fearful, and awkward. And to offer practical ways to pray with people and share the Gospel.

Not because I have it all figured out, but because I know the One who does. I have seen how God has taken my "yes" and transformed shame into joy by His abundant grace. I now carry the privilege of praying for people and sharing the Gospel on some of the world's most beautiful beaches, where once I sought escape, I now stand with a mission on the shores of grace.

The beach did not free my soul; God did!

> **"But thank God! He has made us his captives and continues to lead us along in Christ's triumphal procession. Now he uses us to spread the knowledge of Christ everywhere, like a sweet perfume."**
> **2 Corinthians 2:14 NLT**

Chapter Three
The Power of Prayer

**"The greatest tragedy in life is the prayers
that go unanswered because they go unasked."
~Mark Batterson**

Discovering a New Way to Pray

We had only been living in our Gulf Coast town for a few months when I joined several small groups at our church—each one uniquely stretching me. One group did a short but powerful study on the prayer of Jabez:

> **"Oh, that You would bless me indeed,
> and enlarge my territory,
> that Your hand would be with me,
> and that You would keep me from evil,
> that I may not cause pain."
> (1 Chronicles 4:10 NKJV)**

Praying a scripture like this—asking God to bless me and increase my territory—was different from the prayers I had prayed in the past. I had always believed God would bless, but now was learning it wasn't just something He did occasionally—it was His very nature. And with that, I was learning how to pray in alignment with that truth.

That scripture became my daily prayer for Joey, our family, and me. I asked God to reveal His purpose, expand my thinking, and enlarge my territory for the sake of the Kingdom. I prayed for increased faith and a deeper understanding of His will.

Like a kid in a candy store, I couldn't stop grabbing hold of every truth from God I could find. I was drawn to His presence in a way I'd never experienced. Overwhelmed by the sweetness of His Spirit, worship became a daily craving. It wasn't forced or dutiful—it was like breathing—something I could not live without. After living so long without this connection with God, I couldn't get enough of His love. It was unexplainable!

Praying Through a Pandemic

Then, in the late winter of 2020, the world changed. COVID-19 arrived like an uninvited guest, bringing fear, isolation, and uncertainty. Businesses shut their doors. Grocery stores and gas stations were among the few businesses that remained open. With so many losing their jobs, fear was like a thick fog that settled over people's hearts. Once-busy streets were eerily quiet—even the beaches were closed. That was utterly bizarre.

Amid the chaos, isolation, and uncertainty, I clung to prayer, which kept my spirit anchored.

One day, my close friend, neighbor, and prayer warrior, Gretel, suggested something unexpected: walking through a large outdoor shopping center, that had closed temporarily to pray over every store. The idea intrigued me. I had never done anything like that before.

I wondered, *How exactly would we do it? Would we stop at every door? What do I pray over so many stores?*

Still, I went in faith. With over one hundred stores in the plaza, it felt daunting—so many businesses and unknown needs. But we invited God to work through us as His vessels. I remember praying that every employee and family member of every store would be protected from the virus. We prayed, believing each store would reopen and thrive like never before. We prayed that every person who would one day walk through those doors would receive eternal life. That's a lot of people! I had never prayed so boldly before.

Expanding My Vision

My vision for praying and intercession was expanding. Scripture says to ask anything in His name, and it will be done. My faith was rising supernaturally, and that Saturday morning, as I stepped out, God multiplied my words and increased my belief. That's just who He is. God's supernatural work operates beyond human reasoning. I can't explain it, but I was learning to walk by faith, drawn by His love, and He was doing a deep work in my heart.

I remember looking at all the stores ahead of and behind us, amazed at how long we had been praying. But we didn't stop—we pressed on to finish what we came to accomplish.

Through my prayers to increase my territory for Him, He opened doors I never could have opened on my own. It wasn't me; it was Him. He led the way, using people to position me for His purpose. He was increasing my thoughts to think higher and deeper because His ways are far beyond mine.

Divine Friendships and Daily Walks

We began walking daily during the lockdowns, and soon a neighbor, Renee, joined us. She also became a close friend and a powerful voice for God. Looking back, I see how the Lord had set both Gretel and Renee in place ahead of time—divinely appointed voices of truth and reason, speaking what I was seeking. They brought encouragement, Scripture, and the kind of friendship that felt like a gift from heaven. I had never experienced anything like it in my life—women who walked closely with God, stood on the Word, and walked alongside me as I healed from things I didn't know that I needed to be healed from. It was through this process that I got to know my Savior.

By late spring, our world was still locked down. It was uncertain we would ever live normally again. Gretel phoned with an invitation: to join a few people from our church circling the nearby hospital in prayer—lifting patients and staff to the Lord. About ten of us came, including a young family with children in strollers and praise music from a Bluetooth speaker. The Spirit of God was among us.

After brief introductions, the leader began to pray. What she said made me open my eyes in surprise. She declared the armor of God over each of us—placing the helmet of salvation upon our heads, the breastplate of righteousness over our hearts, the belt of truth around our waists, and the shoes of the Gospel of peace, the sword of the Spirit, and the shield of faith. She prayed with bold authority. I was captivated—I didn't recall anything like that ever before.

As I listened, my heart began to ignite. God revealed Himself in powerful new ways, and my faith grew stronger with each word. I felt as though He was wrapping me in His presence. He was preparing me for a journey I didn't know was coming.

Later, I learned that the passage was found in *Ephesians 6:10-17*. Declaring the armor of God is like putting on God Himself. We are in a spiritual battle, and the truth that victory had been won through the blood of Jesus suddenly made sense to me. The dots were being connected through His Word.

I continued seeking God, His Word, His presence, and His truth.

Confronting Pride and Surrendering Control

A few months later, I attended a weekend conference called *Freedom* with a friend. I told her as we got out of the car, "Let's go get Free!" The first subject they talked about was pride, which I was certain didn't apply to me. I'd always been praised for being independent and strong-willed. Over time, that "strength" was disguised behind a mask as pride, which I thought was good—until I realized it was keeping me from truly knowing God.

No one will tell me what to do!

My need to control every outcome dulled God's voice.

I told her with a confident chuckle, "I probably don't need prayer for this,"—But as they read the traits of pride, conviction hit—

spiritually speaking. My eyes were opened, and I felt the goodness and kindness of God leading me to repentance. Not the "I'm-sorry-God-I'll-eventually-get-it-right" kind of repentance. Not the "I'm sorry, I'm only human" type either. This was complete surrender—laying it at the cross–confessing with my mouth—all the hurts that needed forgiving. Something broke in me. A real heart change. Wow! Talk about leaving my baggage with Jesus. Who knew surrender would feel this way?!

Healing from Past Wounds

I also didn't realize I had carried past wounds into my new life. Time alone doesn't heal heart wounds or shame. It only softens the sting. Keeping pain locked inside had held me hostage to a negative mindset. When I confessed pride to the Lord with a member of the prayer team, I wept in front of a large cross in the church. Throughout the two-day conference, I also confessed rejection, shame, fear, and harboring unforgiveness. With each step, my heart opened wide, and God moved in. I was free!

I had never seen anything like it—over 200 people pouring out their hearts to God, having real "come-to-Jesus" moments.

Pouring Out the Old to Make Room for the New

After that weekend, I craved more of God. I wanted to make room in my life for everything He wanted to do in and through me. I didn't know what that would look like, but I knew there was something that wasn't serving me anymore: alcohol.

Then old mindsets tried to reason with me: *"But wait…I barely drink anymore. Is it really necessary to stop completely? I'll only keep it around for the occasional gathering."*

Since the age of 16, alcohol had stolen my peace, robbed me of clarity, and quieted the voice of God. Drinking had been my source for so many years—happy, sad, mad, or glad. And honestly, I didn't need a reason: I just loved it. So, I asked myself, *"Why am I still clinging to something that steals—even a little—of what God wants to give me in full?"*

My passion was to release that version of myself so God could do a new thing.

One morning, I walked right into the kitchen and poured every drop of alcohol down the sink. Not because God demanded it, but because alcohol had lost its grip on me. I wanted God to have full access to every part of me.

Alcohol took up destructive space in my life, causing emotional, relational, financial, physical, and spiritual harm to me for decades. When I released it, God opened a door I never saw coming: an invitation to pray, encourage, and support women recovering from addiction.

Called to Love

I was so excited because I had carried a deep desire to make a difference in women's lives in that capacity, but I never knew how to act on it. I had once believed my story disqualified me. Instead, God used my surrender as a bridge to pray and care for His daughters.

A second blessing through that ministry was when I met Diane, who became my dear friend, mentor, and spiritual sister. We've often joked that we are like peanut butter and jelly—fitting very well together in ministry. Serving alongside her has brought me deep joy, growth, and the blessing of witnessing our Father's love redeeming the broken lives of God's girls.

I remember God opening that door and feeling overwhelmed with so much gratitude and excitement as God led me there. I then found myself asking, "How, Lord? How do I do this?"

His answer was clear and simple, "Just love."

In the Kingdom, even introductions are divine—God aligns moments, people, and purpose for redemption. Heaven always goes before us, setting up divine appointments to draw hearts back to Him, because in the end, it's all about loving people.

Chapter Four
Stretch Your Faith

**"Faith begins where your
comfort zone ends."
~Christine Caine**

A Stirring in the Spirit

For so long, I believed I had little to offer—either to God or to anyone else. But something was shifting in me big time. God was awakening a new level of creativity in me.

During a simple book study on *"The Circle Maker"* by Mark Batterson, I was challenged to pray bigger, bolder prayers. As I read, something stirred in my heart. *What if I literally walked this out?*

I began to envision a weekly walking group—women circling our community in prayer, praying the Word, declaring God's will, and praying for others we might encounter.

It became a passion inside of me. Group studies are great, but I felt a need I can't explain—to take Christ outside the walls.

When God Confirms the Call

Then the devil would whisper in my ear, *"Who are you to do something like this? You're not a leader."* But I sought God in prayer, and those lies began to crumble. It wasn't a one-and-done prayer moment—it was (and still is) a daily surrender.

During that season of seeking God, I ran into my friend, Mindy. We discovered the Holy Spirit had spoken to both of us about the same things. The more we talked, the more we realized we were meant to form a group. Our hearts and visions aligned. It felt like the territory God had given me was expanding.

One evangelist who inspires me is Todd White—a former addict and atheist, who boldly and lovingly shares Jesus everywhere he goes. He *lives* the gospel out loud— unapologetically: in the streets, restaurants, concerts—anywhere people are.

I mentioned Todd White to Mindy, and she said, "What! No way. I'm reading his testimony right now! I love him!"

We both laughed, knowing that was our confirmation.

Stretch Your Faith Begins

After more prayer, we both sensed the same word from the Holy Spirit: "Stretch." We started a group called *Stretch Your Faith*. We began prayer-walking—walking through specific places while lifting the needs of our community to God. We prayed at schools, beaches, malls, boardwalks, and trails. We covered our church, interceding for our pastor, staff, and volunteers. We circled fire stations, parks, and neighborhoods in prayer, believing that every step we took was an act of faith, bringing His presence into the heart of each place and asking God to draw people to Jesus.

Before we set out, we prayed for divine encounters—opportunities to pray for healing, share the gospel, and simply be a light.

Encounters on the Path

The first person we met was a young woman on a walking trail. Starting with a casual conversation, we asked if she lived nearby. She stated she was from the area, but at a crossroads in her life and had to make tough decisions. Unsure of what to do, she was confused and went for a walk to clear her head. I asked, "How can we pray for you?"

She was comforted by those words and asked if we could pray about her next steps. Mindy prayed precisely what she needed to hear. The young woman was so touched she began to cry and couldn't believe we just prayed for her right there on a walking path.

Here's the truth: When you step out in faith to pray for a perfect stranger, you intend to bless them, but in the process, you receive an even more incredible blessing: the joy of obedience, the presence of God moving through you, and the stretching of your own faith.

Going Deeper: Prayers on the Beach

Every week, we prayed and asked God for wisdom on a new area to saturate with prayer. Each week brought a new surprise—and an area God would highlight for prayer. We expected God to move mightily, and He did!

One beautiful fall day in October, we met at one of the public beaches. We felt the Holy Spirit was prompting us to step out further. What did that look like? We decided to split into pairs and walk along the beach in different directions, praying as we went, just as Jesus sent out his disciples in pairs.

We prayed and covered our families with heaven's presence, our community, each other, and those walking the beach—growing bolder with every step. Through this, I learned to pray out loud with confidence and clarity, staying open to whoever God led us to.

When Obedience Feels Scary

We set a time to come back together, share our experiences, and pray for each other before leaving. That day, a newcomer joined us —a young, single mom of three in desperate need of prayer. The compassion we all felt for her was undeniable, and as we surrounded her in prayer, she admitted she was addicted to prescription meds. She desperately wanted to be free from them. Our hearts broke with hers.

As one of the group leaders, I knew I might be the one to lead this prayer, but fear gripped me. I looked at my friend Gretel, thinking, *She's stronger than I. She should do it.*

My mind still had me stuck, believing I didn't have what it took to lead this prayer. I had prayed corporately with others for people to be freed from this or that, but I had never *led* that type of prayer.

I looked at Gretel and said, "I don't know …."

She interrupted and spoke, "You got this. Jesus is with you."

I felt like she gently pushed the baby bird out of the nest, and I'm so grateful she did.

I stepped forward and laid my hands on the young woman. Everyone joined in. Together, we lifted her need God for her healing.

Freedom and Faithfulness

Weeks later, she testified that, with God's help and her doctor's support, she had been tapering off her doses. Then came the breakthrough—she was completely free! She was deeply thankful to the Lord for her healing.

Let me be clear: healing is not up to me or anyone else. All God needs is a willing vessel: someone who believes, who trusts Him, and is willing to stretch their faith.

Walk It Out

Even if you're afraid—do it anyway.
God will give you the words.
You don't need to sound eloquent.
You only need a heart that loves His people.
What begins in obedience becomes a love story—
One etched in grace along every path. Love leads the way!

Chapter Five
It Only Takes a Spark

"He said to His disciples,
'The harvest is plentiful but the workers are few.
So pray to the Lord who is in charge of the harvest; ask Him
to send more workers into His fields.'"
Matthew 9:37-38 NLT

A Movie That Sparked a Movement

Have you seen the movie *Jesus Revolution*? If not, I highly recommend it. This film is more than just a story—it's a powerful depiction of how a single spark ignited a movement of God that swept across the country. Its impact was truly revolutionary!

My husband and I were part of a couple's small group that saw that movie in January 2023. By the time the credits rolled, we were all deeply inspired to share Christ more boldly. Not long after, our small group leaders, Bruce and Leigha, shared that they felt the Holy Spirit nudging them to set up a prayer tent on the beach. When they said that, a fire was ignited in me—I knew I had to be part of it!

We all caught the vision: a huge harvest of souls was here, right on the sand, ready to be loved, prayed over, and introduced to the Gospel.

Launching Souls on the Sand

The prayer tent became a reality in March of 2023—just in time for spring break! We gathered to pray for wisdom and direction for what God would do. We had so much fun preparing—from ordering silicone scripture bracelets and Bibles to brainstorming creative ideas. We placed stickers with scriptures on water bottles for the cooler. One of the ladies in our group came up with the name "Souls on the Sand." The creativity was electric. The vision was taking wings.

Leigha, along with Sandra, another member of our group, suggested a thoughtful, simple idea—small paintbrushes for beachgoers to brush the sand off their feet. It was a great idea, and while it was practical, it also became a symbol of care and welcome. A few artistic members hand-painted the brush handles in soft pastels. Some added tiny palm trees or colorful flip-flops on one side and a short scripture on the other—powerful reminders of God's love. Everyone wanted one (or two!).

Meeting People Where They Are

We also laid out laminated copies of the *Romans Road*—a pathway through Scripture that walks people through salvation, using verses from the book of Romans. At this time, I had heard of it but wasn't familiar enough to guide someone through the verses. To make it even more accessible, a QR code was added, allowing people to scan and explore the verses online. (*A full version of the Romans Road, is included in the appendix.*)

These little touches may seem small, but each intentionally said, "You are noticed. You are cared for. You are loved, and God is reaching for you."

With the words "Pray Here" written in bold purple, we set up the tent area with Bibles, bracelets, praise music, and water bottles. Leigha once said that handing out water reminded her of the woman at the well—she came for physical water, but Jesus gave her Living Water.

Beachgoers come to enjoy a relaxing day away from work and stress, and may wonder—*How can prayer help me today?*

They leave with a different experience than expected. It's so miraculous how God works.

Simple Questions Open Big Doors

People don't always know how to ask for prayer. Sometimes they're with friends, and it feels awkward. They may want prayer, but are hesitant to approach us. That's why we began with friendly greetings and simple questions like: "Good morning! Are you visiting here?"

We introduce ourselves and offer water, bracelets, and little 'Jesus Loves You' figurines, which are a big hit for everyone. These small acts of kindness make all the difference. People respond when they feel we care. This allows for easy and authentic conversation without pressure.

I've learned people are more open than I once believed. The Spirit of God opens doors that I could never open on my own. He just does it.

Miracles on the Sand

Beachgoers came by for encouragement, healing, freedom from addiction, and salvation—and sometimes, they prayed for us. I'll never forget when children prayed for us; it touched the hearts of everyone.

At noon, we gathered to pray for our country—not with any political agenda, but simply for God's protection over our nation and its leaders. People who are uncomfortable asking for personal prayers had the courage to come together and pray for our country as a group.

That spring and summer, I witnessed something extraordinary: humanity uniting and religious walls breaking down. It was more powerful than anything I could have ever imagined, and I was hungry for more.

Our hearts longed to show the matchless love and mercy of Jesus Christ. Again and again, we saw God working in the hearts of those who came to the beach to escape life's burdens, only to encounter something far greater.

Simple Conversations Plant Seeds

I'll never forget a man who came to the tent. His wife, two high schoolers, and one of their friends sat nearby in their beach chairs. He kept coming back to talk. During one conversation, he said, "This is so cool what you are doing. I am a Christian and never considered doing anything like this back home."

We never know what seeds God is planting in the hearts of others when they go back home. But we know it's not about us. It's all about God—who He is, and what He's doing through us.

The Power of Showing Up

Prayer Tents allow us to meet people right where they are—often in their most relaxed state. Sometimes it's as simple as a warm greeting, a blessing for safe travel, or a kind word. Other times, the brokenness rises to the surface, and hearts open in unexpected ways.

Sometimes, we share the Good News—the Gospel. Other times, we pray for encouragement or lay hands on them for physical healing. But above all, we simply love—without pressure or fear. We want people to see Christians not as those to be avoided, but as individuals who genuinely care.

I have learned people are hungry to know someone truly cares. When a stranger prays for physical healing, speaks encouragement over them, or offers a hug, it can open their heart in a way that sermons sometimes can't.

The love that points to Jesus is hard to ignore. And when healing prayers open a door, it often leads to something greater—an invitation to a relationship with Jesus.

Learning to Share the Gospel

Participating in the prayer tent stretched my faith in ways I never imagined. It was total reliance on God to hear the needs of the people. It took courage and the belief that God could and would use me. I had to come out of my shell. It took a mustard seed of faith, but that was enough.

Every week, fear was replaced with boldness, and hesitation was replaced with compassion. But it wasn't just about faith, trust, and obedience—it was fun! I could not wait to share Jesus.

Even as I grew more comfortable approaching people for prayer, I struggled to share the Gospel. We can pray big, beautiful prayers and believe for healing, but if we walk away from that and don't share with them how to know Jesus and seek forgiveness, we've missed the very thing Romans 1:16 tells us—the Gospel is the power of God that brings salvation to everyone who believes.

So, what's our hang-up with the actual Gospel? Is it a lack of knowledge, or that we never hear anyone say it—unless it's the Pastor in the pulpit on Sunday? There must be a simple way to explain this.

I would ask those I was talking to, "Is Jesus your Lord and Savior?" If they said yes, that was awesome, praise God! If they said no, I'd ask them if they wanted to know how to invite Him into their hearts, and then we'd say a prayer. But to be honest, I was stopping short of explaining the full Gospel.

What is the Gospel?

Have you ever shared the Gospel or wondered how to share the Gospel?

The Gospel is the Good News of how God stepped into humanity and entered our sinful world as a baby, to rescue us from our sin, sickness, death, and eternal separation from our Father God. We could not save ourselves, so God sent His Son, Jesus, to save us. The law did not, and will not, save anyone. Only the sinless blood of Jesus can do that.

We are called to share this truth. We must have a heart for the lost and a willingness to share the way back to God with them through Jesus.

This book exists in part to help Christians feel more confident sharing the Gospel, with love and clarity. There are many ways to introduce someone to Jesus. Several are included in the Appendix, but what matters most is showing up, being present, and letting God do the rest.

Final Spark: A Sacred Surprise

What began as a spark ignited by a movie and a tent became something far more personal. With every prayer, every smile, and every soul we met on the sand, God was refining not just my faith, but my boldness.

And just when I thought I had experienced the best of it, He surprised me again. Because sometimes, the most sacred moments come not in tents, but in unexpected conversations … like a bachelorette party on the beach.

Chapter Six
Here Comes the Bride

**"Glory belongs to God,
whose power is at work in us.
By this power he can do infinitely more
than we can ask or imagine."
(Ephesians 3:20 GW)**

A Divine Appointment in Disguise

No one expected a bachelorette party to feel like a divine appointment—but that's precisely what it became.

When my husband and I joined our group one morning, we went for a walk along the shoreline. We carried cold water and a handful of scripture bracelets, ready to offer to the beachgoers.

On our way back, we met two women walking toward us, and one of them complimented my t-shirt. We slowed down, stepped closer, and I smiled as I thanked her. I offered her my last *Armor of God* bracelet. I introduced my husband and myself, mentioning that we were at the prayer tent just down the beach.

Then I asked, "Where are you from and what brings you here?"

That's when I learned they were mother and daughter from Alabama. The older woman, probably late forties, nodded toward a nearby group of young women and said, "My other daughter is the bachelorette. Her bridesmaids are celebrating her this weekend. Please go pray for them, too," as she laughed sincerely.

I laughed with her and said, "Okay! We'll bring some bracelets."

We prayed for them and went on our way.

Where's the Bride?

Not long after, we spotted the group having a great time—laughing, tanning, and soaking in the moment. A friend and I walked toward them carrying our water bottles and bracelets. As we approached, I called out playfully, "Where's the bride?!"

A young woman stepped forward in a white bathing suit and bridal banner, beaming. She thrust her fists into the air and exclaimed, "I'm right here! Yeah!!"

We introduced ourselves, as her friends excitedly gathered around us, smiling and laughing as they sifted through the bracelets, picking out their favorite colors and Scriptures. Their joy and enthusiasm were contagious. "What's your name?" I asked, matching her excitement.

"Anna," she replied.

I introduced myself and my friend. "We're from the Prayer Tent over there," I said, gesturing toward it. "We just wanted to come say hello—and we'd love to pray for you, if that's ok."

Her eyes instantly filled with tears. "Oh my gosh, that is the sweetest thing. Of course, you can pray!"

I could feel the presence of God.

A Circle of Blessing

The bridesmaids gathered around, their chatter quieted, and we joined hands in a sweet moment.

I asked Anna her fiancé's name. With trembling lips, she responded, "Brandon."

Tears began spilling down her face as the atmosphere shifted in that small space of young women. I prayed, first for her and then for Brandon, and their future together. I also prayed for their friendships, asking God to cover and protect them. My friend followed, praying over their upcoming marriage and the people surrounding them, that every voice would encourage unity and love.

By the time we finished praying, they were all moved because of God's Spirit, and several of the women were wiping their eyes. They hugged us tightly and thanked us, smiling through their tears.

"We never expected anything like this. I will never forget this," the bride whispered. "Thank you so much."

Grace Pulled Up a Chair

We returned to the tent with tears of joy, overwhelmed by the tenderness of what had just happened.

But God was not finished.

A few minutes later, one of the young women from the group—one who had hugged me with tears in her eyes—walked to the tent looking for me. As soon as I saw her, I stepped forward, greeting her.

"Can I share something with you?" she asked softly as her eyes welled up. "What happened over there … it changed me. I know it has. Please don't judge me, but I've been drinking—and I don't want to continue down this path. I was in Cancun last week with my mom, and we were both drinking the whole time. But I want to change."

"I will not judge you," I said gently. "I'm proud of you for coming over here and sharing that with me," as I wrapped her in a warm hug.

She broke down crying.

Shame Meets Truth

I looked her in the eyes, like a momma would a daughter, and I reminded her, "God does not condemn you. He sees you. He loves you. And He is so proud of you for taking this step."

I prayed Scripture because His word is His will. I shared words of life and truth, such as, "God's plans for you are filled with hope and strength—and He calls you to walk in His power. You can do all things through Christ, who gives you strength. He will care for you, lead, restore, and make you new."

I spoke into the places where shame had lived too long. God's presence surrounded us like a blanket. We were both overwhelmed by the depth of His love.

The Ache to Do More

After she left, I sat under the tent, undone—in awe of what God had done…and yet convicted by what I hadn't done.

I was growing more confident—what I like to call *Godfident*—in praying for people and meeting them in their place of need. However, I still froze up when it came to sharing the Gospel.

Not everyone who prays is saved. I knew that. But I didn't always know how to ask the right questions.

- What would I say if someone weren't sure?
- How would I explain salvation clearly?
- Could I invite them into a relationship with Jesus, right there on the sand?

I knew God had this. It wasn't about me. It was about planting seeds. Still, my heart desired to do more than offer a prayer. I wanted to offer eternity with their creator.

We can't remain silent about salvation—too much is at stake.

A Changed Bride—And Me

I kept searching and asking God. I'll get there in this story. But for now, know this: Jesus met a bachelorette at a party on the beach that day—and I didn't leave the same.

Chapter Seven
A Tent Peg in the Sand

"When it is God, even the sand cries out!"
~Caron Caroll

A God Orchestrated Moment

On a beautiful day in July of 2023, my friend Patty and I were at the Prayer tent, along with the others. As we often did, two of us left the tent to walk along the beach and connect with people. We had already prayed for many people on our walk, but we both felt there was one more to pray for.

There, at the same time, we saw her—this young woman sitting by the water's edge. We began walking toward her. And that's when I heard it:

"Pray for her husband."

It stopped me. *Was that me saying that? Could I have made that up? The words had come so quickly, so clearly—there is no way they were mine.* Doubt stepped in. *What if I'm wrong? I think I'll just act like I didn't hear that.*

Unexpected Connection

Those thoughts swirled in my head while we introduced ourselves. We told her we felt led by God to pray for her. We chatted casually for a few moments. She shared that she loved Jesus and loved that we were out praying. In our conversation, I discovered she is from my home state, Arkansas. She owns a second home at the beach and makes frequent trips here.

An instant bond was formed. It felt as if we had known each other for years.

Then she mentioned that she knew of a group with a prayer tent on another beach, a few minutes away—the very group I had heard about and hoped to meet one day.

A Bold Step of Obedience

As we were wrapping up our conversation, Patty had a powerful word for her. We all prayed and felt like we were old friends reuniting.

But as we were walking away, the words I had heard came back.

"Pray for her husband."

I had to pray as God told me. If I was wrong—I was wrong.

"Wait," I said. "I think I'm supposed to pray for your husband. I don't know if you are married or want to be, but that's what I heard. Is that okay?"

She lit up with a big smile. "Sure!" though she did not give me any details.

So, I prayed. We hugged. We exchanged numbers. And we even took a selfie. It felt like God had knit something special together in just a few moments.

The Sign Beneath the Sand

Patty and I were on a spiritual high as we walked back to the tent. God's presence was so real and tangible. When we returned, we joined the others in a circle and shared our stories, running our toes through the sand as we listened. The atmosphere was joyful, even majestic, as we celebrated what God had done through each of us.

Suddenly, one of the women felt something hard beneath the sand. Her husband reached down and pulled it up.

"It's a tent peg," he said.

A tent peg? Something stirred in me. I knew there was a scripture about that—something about enlarging territory. I couldn't quite place it, but suddenly I blurted out:

"A tent peg!? That means God is increasing our tent pegs! He is enlarging our tent!"

I knew it meant expansion, but I was unsure of the details. I just knew there was a message in that tent peg.

That feeling, that scene … it stayed with me. Later that evening, I looked up the scripture:

"Enlarge the place of your tent,
And let them stretch out the curtains
of your dwellings;
Do not spare;
Lengthen your cords,
And strengthen your stakes."
(Isaiah 54:2 NKJV)

The NLT version says it like this:

"Enlarge your house; build an addition. Spread out
your home, and spare no expense!"

I love the next verse!

"For you will soon be bursting at the seams.
Your descendants will occupy other nations
and resettle the ruined cities."
(Isaiah 54:3 NKJV)

This scripture speaks metaphorically of God's promises to bless, expand, and establish His Kingdom through us and our descendants on earth. It's generational. And that tent peg—buried in the sand—was His reminder. A sign. A promise.

Wow! It all came together.

The tent peg in the sand wasn't just a coincidence. It was confirmation. He was expanding our territory—spiritually and literally.

God really can speak through anything—even tent pegs.

Chapter Eight
Has Anyone Ever Prayed for You?

"Being prayed for is often the moment someone finally feels seen by heaven."
~Anonymous

A Generation Hungry for Heaven

Have you ever wondered how many people walk through life never hearing their name whispered in prayer? Never having someone stand beside them, calling heaven down on their behalf?

God was stirring my heart to pray for the younger generation, to open my eyes to something deeper— because they are hungry. Hungry for truth. For connection. For someone to care.

His Divine Set Ups

One morning, I arrived at the prayer tent much earlier than usual. As I approached, I noticed a young, blonde woman kneeling in prayer on the sand. She stood as I walked toward her and introduced herself as Katie. The moment we met, I knew exactly who she was; the woman I had heard about who led the prayer tent on the beach a few minutes from there. She told me she rarely comes to this part of the beach.

Only God could have orchestrated this.

"I prayed for one of your friends last week," I told her.

Katie's face lit up. "Oh, did you pray for her husband?" she asked.

"Yes! How do you know that?" I laughed.

"Because she called me bawling right after you left," Katie said. "The night before you prayed, we had a 'How to pray' workshop at the chapel. I challenged them to pray bolder prayers. She had asked for prayer to meet her husband—and then you came up the next day and you said exactly that!"

In that moment, I felt an undeniable sense of awe before God. He cared so deeply for this one woman that He used a stranger on the beach to confirm His love by hearing her prayers and knowing her heart's desire. But He wasn't just working in her life—He was teaching me to trust Him when I hear His voice. Words of knowledge are revelations straight from His heart.

> **"For to one is given by the Spirit
> the word of wisdom;
> to another the word of knowledge
> by the same Spirit."
> (1 Corinthians 12:8 KJV)**

Meeting Katie that day led to a coffee date. She shared her bold faith journey, which her husband and she were called to. I learned their mission was to reach Gen Z with the gospel—right there on the beaches of a small coastal community. They had five tents set up for one week at Spring Break and another at Fall Break, each with a simple question: "Need Prayer?"

Her passion and enthusiasm were contagious. I felt a heart connection deep within—God was actively moving my tent pegs! I wanted to go deeper with Him. I wanted to be a part of sharing His abundant grace and love.

So, I joined her prayer team.

From the moment I stepped into the tent, I was overwhelmed by the crowds of people who would come for prayer. Young adults approached with friends, unashamed and hungry for more. I could feel their longing for something real—a connection with Jesus.

What surprised me most? The number of young men coming for prayer. They were open. Uninhibited and honest, they shared their hearts. There weren't just a few; there were young men repeatedly seeking prayer. Some were battling addictions to alcohol or struggling with lust. Others needed prayer for direction in their lives or were grieving the loss of a friend to suicide. Young and old requested prayer for family members to be saved, to draw closer to God, for marriages to be restored, for relief from sickness, and direction in life. Many didn't know exactly what they needed; they were just open to prayer.

In a beautiful exchange, some young men even prayed for us!

It wasn't just students—people of all ages stopped. Some sped past the tent on their bikes, only to hit the brakes and turn around, drawn by something greater. Drivers honked and waved as they passed. Some even gave a thumbs-up in agreement with what God was doing.

I was overwhelmed by God's love and the joy of witnessing His love, meet them where they were. The red tent stood as a beacon of hope.

The Power of a Single Prayer

Katie visited each tent across the small beach community during the several-day outreach. One afternoon, as she walked to our tent, a few young women strolled by. She asked if we could pray for them. They said, "Yes." But her next question opened my eyes to the importance of these tents. It's not just about prayer but about connection.

She gently asked, **"Has anyone ever prayed for you before?"**

Drawn by her sincerity, they moved closer and chuckled nervously, "Not really."

I recognized how common it is for people to have never had a prayer uttered, especially for themselves. I felt something touch my heart so sweetly, as she ministered to them like a mother to her beloved daughters.

Seen, Loved, and Remembered

The tenderness of this moment caused me to flash back to the moments in my youth when I was being prayed for at summer camp. I felt noticed and loved.

Prayer can create an atmosphere of intimacy in the heart of the one receiving prayer, whether you see it or not, and supernaturally, those hearts become softened. It happened to me.

Reaching out in love to a world that's hurting isn't optional; it's essential.

When you pray for someone, it's a call to heaven to reach their heart, touch their pain, and remind them that they are seen, loved, and not forgotten. Prayer brings hope and connection. We are the ones connecting them to God. Isn't that awesome?!

> **"But how can they call on him**
> **to save them unless they believe in him?**
> **And how can they believe in him**
> **if they have never heard about him?**
> **And how can they hear about him**
> **unless someone tells them?"**
> **(Romans 10:14-15 NLT)**

For all we know, we may be the first ones who have ever prayed for them. While most people welcome prayer, some don't.

And that's okay, I've learned not to take it personally. Even a simple offer that is rejected can plant a seed. If God's Word is spoken, it won't return void. Seeds are planted and will accomplish something —even if it isn't evident right then.

People are desperate to know Jesus, even if they don't realize it. But how will they know unless someone tells them?

A Silent Cry for Hope

Prayer ignites angelic activity. It invites the will of God to invade people's lives.

I often look at crowds and silently wonder:

Do they need prayer?
Do they know how much they are loved?
What are they struggling with?
What wounds might they carry?
What are their fears?
Could they use an encouraging word today?

What if today, I get to be the one who leads them one step closer to freedom? I am not a counselor or a therapist, but I can pray. And that is enough—because Jesus takes care of the rest.

Final Word: You CAN Be the One

The world is starving for hope.

And we carry it.

They may never know the Hope we know, unless someone asks, **"How can we pray for you?"**

Chapter Nine
The Good Person

"God saved you by his grace when you believed.
And you can't take credit for this; it is a gift from God.
Salvation is not a reward for the good things we have done,
so none of us can boast about it."
(Ephesians 2:8-9 NLT)

A Common Measure of Goodness

Most people consider themselves to be genuinely good people, or at least "good enough." They measure their goodness by comparing themselves to others, highlighting moral behavior, or recalling the good things they strive to do. The average person tends to assume their heart is in the right place.

But how do we truly measure goodness? That's where the moral law comes in. It's not just a list of rules—it's God's measuring stick, revealing whether someone is "good enough." *Good enough for what?* To meet the standard set by God Himself, as revealed in the Ten Commandments.

"We are all infected and impure with sin.
When we display our righteous deeds,
they are nothing but filthy rags.
Like autumn leaves,
we wither and fall, and our sins
sweep us away like the wind."

Even our very best efforts fall short. Apart from God, even our most noble deeds cannot cleanse us. Only through the righteousness of Christ can we be made clean.

So, how does the Good News intersect with this reality?

I began learning by listening to an evangelist, Ray Comfort, who uses the moral law to help people recognize their need for a Savior. He often begins with simple, revealing questions, such as, "Have you ever told a lie?"

Of course, we all have. Every one of us has fallen short of God's perfect standard—but that's just the beginning of sharing the gospel.

Stepping into Evangelism

In November 2023, I joined my church's evangelism team. We would head out to local outdoor shopping centers in the evenings. Honestly, I was nervous—not heart-racing fear, but fear of man, fear of stumbling over my words, fear of not knowing the Scriptures. Yet at the same time, I was so excited to get there, knowing God saw me stepping out in obedience and was equipping me as I went. (He was excited for me, too!)

That first night, I only knew a few people. We gathered in the parking lot, prayed, and formed small groups of two to three. Most of the group were young adults, passionate and bold in their faith.

I was the oldest and least experienced, but I knew I was right where I should be. Their courage inspired me.

Spirit-Led Moments

We began with our usual conversation starters. Simple, ordinary moments with people became opportunities for us to connect with the Holy Spirit, who was leading us.

One evening, three of us were walking around, and I saw a couple walking toward us. Stepping out, I said, "Hello, are you guys from here?"

They smiled and replied, "No, we are from Missouri."

We chatted briefly before I invited them to answer a few simple faith-based questions from a questionnaire. They agreed to participate.

Most people enjoy engaging with others and answering questions.

The Surprising Encounter

The first question was, "Do you go to church or practice any religion?" Neither one identified as a Christian. He declared himself an atheist.

Suddenly, the weight of the conversation hit me. I got nervous. *How am I—or we—going to communicate faith with someone who doesn't even believe God exists?*

Still, I sensed God's quiet assurance to keep going, "Would you consider yourself a good person?"

Both quickly answered, "Yes."

I followed up with, "What do you believe happens when you die?"

The man shared his belief in reincarnation. The woman agreed that she believed in reincarnation but added that she still believed in God.

As we continued, one of our group shared a Scripture:

"We die only once, and then we are judged."
(Hebrews 9:27 CEV)

This verse opened a deeper conversation about eternity—that there are no cycles of rebirth, but rather one life, followed by standing before God.

No Arguments, Just Truth and Love

The woman was engaged, and her heart was opening to hearing the truth. Her partner joined in and shared his unique perspective on life—he was intriguing, even though we didn't get a chance to share much about God.

We didn't argue. We didn't debate. We simply shared what the Bible said and extended love and grace to them.

These are important keys to remember.

Before we parted ways, I asked if we could pray for him to have a personal encounter with God. To my surprise, he said yes.

That simple yes was powerful. It may have seemed small, but in God's eyes, even the tiniest opening can be the start of something eternal.

Even if he had said no, we would have still prayed for him later—and we did! That's the beautiful thing about prayer—no one can stop your prayers.

The Seeds We Sow

As we walked away, I was deeply encouraged. Evangelism isn't about winning an argument or checking a box. It's about planting seeds, trusting the Holy Spirit to water them, and remembering that every person—no matter how they answer—is deeply loved by God.

I left that night more convinced than ever:

God doesn't call the equipped—**He equips the called. And even in my fear and inadequacy, His love is always enough.**

Chapter Ten
Bold as a Lion

**"This is my command—
Be strong and courageous!
Do not be afraid or discouraged.
For the LORD your God
goes before you wherever you go."
(Joshua 1:9 NLT)**

Doubts and a Nudge

As we shared hope with people one evening at our familiar outdoor marketplace, I spotted a young couple and nudged Cherie, the outreach and evangelism leader from my church. She's bold and never afraid to share God's Word in truth and love.

"Let's go talk to them," I said.

But as we started walking their way, doubt crept in. I remembered being their age—putting on confidence like a mask and hiding behind attitude. Looking at them, I thought, *there's no way they'll talk to us. They'll probably walk off before we even say two words.*

There go those thoughts again. Stop it!

Right then, I was convicted by the Holy Spirit, and I was quickly shown that you cannot judge a book by its cover.

A Surprising Yes

We approached them with a smile and introduced ourselves. I asked, "Are you visiting or are you from around here?"

They said they lived locally.

"Are you in high school?" I followed up.

"Yeah, we're sixteen," they answered.

"We're from a local church," I told them, "And we're out here praying for people. "Can we pray for you?"

The guy quickly said, "Yes, you can," and she nodded.

Before we prayed, I asked, "Can I ask you something? Do you go to church?" I wanted to sense where they were spiritually so we could really speak to their hearts.

He said, "Not right now."

Cherie jumped in, straight to the point. "Have you ever heard the gospel?"

He looked puzzled. "I'm not sure."

Cherie turned to the girl, who quietly said, "No."

The Gospel—Plain and Clear

Without hesitation or intimidation, Cherie began sharing the truth.

> "God created Adam and Eve and placed them in the Garden. But when Adam disobeyed God, sin entered

the world and separated all of us from Him. That separation still exists, but because God loves us, He sent His Son, Jesus, to pay for our sins with His own blood. Jesus restored what was broken, and through Him, we can be made right with God again. The Bible says, 'We've all sinned and fallen short of God's glory.' But God made a way back."

Cherie looked at him and asked, "Have you ever heard any of this before?"

The young man shook his head. "Not that clearly."

"Would you like to ask Jesus to forgive your sins and be your Savior and Lord?" Cherie continued.

Tears welled up in his eyes. "This is what I've been looking for," he said.

He was ready to surrender to Jesus! His friend nodded in agreement. Behind a façade of hardness and toughness were tender hearts ready for someone to bring them hope.

The Power of a Yes

What if I had been with someone else, and we chickened out? It's not about our fears and feelings—it's about their eternity—and that's the mindset we must keep.

But look what God did! You just never know. That's why we go. Listen to that voice that says, *"This one."* Be as bold as lions.

The world is full of people who are hungry for truth, aching for hope, and seeking something genuine. No one is too far gone. Jesus died for everyone.

We don't save anyone—that's God's job.

But we must be willing to step out and share the Good News.

You never know who's ready to receive it…until you go.

Eternity is on the Other Side of Your Yes

From personal experience, I want to encourage you in this: Every time you step past your doubts, God will show you that He is always working. He only asks for your yes. And when you say "yes," you become part of His rescue mission—one heart at a time.

That's why we go.

That's why we pray.

That's why we share.

Chapter Eleven
A Gift We Can't Earn

**"We bring nothing to our salvation,
except the sin that made it necessary"
~Jonathan Edwards**

A Conversation at the Mall

One night at the mall, after I had been going out for several months, I noticed two women walking in our direction. As we drew closer, I sensed God nudging me: 'Talk to them.'

I smiled and asked, "Hey there, are you ladies from here?"

Questions out of the blue tend to catch people off guard like, *I know what you're thinking, who are you, and why are you asking me that?*

But I just kept talking, and they forgot it was weird. I asked where they were from and if they were enjoying their vacation.

We introduced ourselves and shared why we felt led to stop— because we believe every encounter is a divine appointment.

"We are from a local church and are out praying for people tonight. How can we pray for you?" I asked.

They responded, "Maybe just safe travels going home."

"Okay, definitely!" I spoke. "Can I ask you a question before we pray?"

"Sure," they both replied.

"One of these days, you will die and face the Father in Heaven. When He asks why He should let you in, what will you say?" I asked sincerely.

The first one said confidently, "Because I belong to Jesus."

The other one chuckled nervously, "Well … I don't think He would."

I asked, "Why do you believe that?"

She answered honestly, "Because I have made terrible decisions. There's probably no way I'm going to heaven. I'm not good enough."

Why We All Need a Savior

With sincerity, I said, "You know, none of us is good enough." There's a scripture that says, "No one is righteous—not even one" (Romans 3:10 NLT).

That means that no one is righteous because of what we do or don't do—we will never be good enough for a Holy God. But because God loves us so much, He sent His Son, Jesus, to die for us and pay for our sins with His own blood. He paid the debt we couldn't pay.

I continued, "Jesus saw the mess we were in, and He left Heaven to rescue us. We've all broken God's law, but Jesus paid our fine. That's why He went to the cross."

She seemed amazed and nodded slowly, as if the truth was settling into her soul, saying she understood what I told her.

"Is it ok if I ask you a few deeper questions based on God's laws?

"Sure," she replied.

"Have you ever told a lie?"

She laughed out loud and said, "Yes."

"Have you ever stolen anything, even something small, or looked at another person with lust?"

"Yes," she said, chuckling.

"So, if you were to be judged today, based on His law, would you be guilty or innocent?" "Heaven or hell?"

Without hesitation, she quietly said, "Hell."

I looked at her with love and assurance. "And that is exactly why Jesus came—for you. He loves you so much, He paid your debt with His life, so you don't have to face that penalty and go to hell. Jesus desires for you to receive His free gift. Tonight's encounter was not random—it was specifically for you, and it's God's invitation to you. He's inviting you into His grace."

The law will never save—redemption came in the flesh, not rules.

The Law Exposes and Grace Redeems

She was deeply moved, so I asked her if she wanted to pray to receive salvation, forgiveness, and make Him her Lord and Savior. She wasn't quite ready to do that. Instead, we prayed He would reveal Himself to her in a new and fresh way.

She was moved and hugged me as we were leaving.

I added, "I press in because it is very possible, I will never see you again this side of heaven, and I want to see you in heaven. I believe we will recognize each other. That's why I share the Gospel—so you'll have the chance to say yes."

As we were finishing up, I handed her a pamphlet that clearly explained God's pathway to salvation, so when she read it, she would know how to respond.

She hugged me again, her gratitude unmistakable.

The Life-Changing Question

Why does the Gospel Matter?

Because every person carries a sin-debt. And unless that debt is paid, it remains outstanding—and eternally costly.

The truth is, we've all broken God's law. Even one violation makes us guilty by His perfect standard. The penalty for sin is death. That's why Jesus is not an option—He is a necessity. He died for guilty sinners like you and me. Not because we deserved it—but because we needed it and we couldn't do it ourselves.

I've learned how crucial it is to help people see two choices we all face:

- We either accept the payment Jesus made for us through His shed blood.

- Or we try to pay for our own sins with religious acts, good deeds, and perfection. Trying to fix ourselves only leads to eternal separation from God.

Some people are ready to hear it boldly; others require a gentler conversation with tender care. I listen carefully, watch body language, and let the Holy Spirit guide me. But one thing remains:

Only the Gospel can set people free—that's the blood of Jesus.

Even people who have been in church their whole lives haven't heard the full truth. The world is crying out for it.

We must be bold in love—but never harsh. Arguing and browbeating with Scriptures won't save anyone. But when we share genuine love, mercy, and authentic compassion, hearts are more likely to open and receive the message.

At the end of the day, the sobering truth is this: The standard isn't "pretty good" or "better than most."

God's law is perfection.

None of us can meet that.

But Jesus did.

And *His* perfect blood was the price we could never pay.

Why His Blood?

People may ask:

"Why did He have to die?"

"Why did His blood pay for our sins?"

I wrote this out to help explain it simply. It helped me, and hopefully it will help others, so they won't feel overwhelmed or lost.

In the Old Testament, God established that sin required a blood sacrifice. Something or someone had to die to pay the price. That's why the blood of animals (usually goats, lambs, or bulls) was offered. The head of the family would bring the best animal to the High Priest. Through that sacrifice, the sins were temporarily paid, but never permanently. Animal blood made payment, or atonement, but could never truly redeem a person.

> **"For the life of the flesh is in the blood,
> And I have given it to you upon the altar to make
> atonement for your souls;
> For it is the blood that makes atonement
> For the soul."
> (Leviticus 17:11 NKJ)**

Redemption means to buy back, to rescue, to free someone from debt. Only Jesus—the spotless, sinless Lamb of God—was able to redeem us eternally. His sacrifice was final because He was and is the only one without sin. His blood is pure. No more animals. No more yearly offerings.

One perfect sacrifice—once and for all.

"When Jesus had tasted it, he said, 'It is finished!'
Then He bowed His head and gave up His Spirit."
(John 19:30 NLT)

My Prayer for You

It's my prayer that as you read this, your confidence to share God's love and truth is growing. We don't step out in our own strength; we step out in **God-fidence.**

Faith is action.

The Holy Spirit empowers us.

He goes before us and prepares hearts before we open our mouths.

People are longing for hope, and we've been called to share it with them.

All God asks of you and me is that we say YES to Him!

Chapter Twelve
Born Again

**"Jesus replied, 'I tell you the truth, unless
you are born again, you cannot see the
Kingdom of God.'"
(John 3:3 NLT)**

One night, a gentleman from my church and I were having a conversation with two young men while out praying. We asked them if they had received Jesus as their Lord and Savior. They confidently answered, "Yes."

As we continued the conversation, we asked them, "So, you are born again?"

They appeared puzzled.

"No? —Well—I'm not sure about that," one of them said.

What Does It Really Mean?

In John 3, Jesus told Nicodemus that being born again is essential to seeing the Kingdom of God. This is a foundational truth when explaining salvation. Faith in Christ isn't just about changing behavior—it's a complete spiritual rebirth.

It's not a physical change but a transformation of the heart. When we invite the Holy Spirit in, He renews us and leads us into the life for which we were created. We become a new person in Christ.

A New Identity

A new identity is given because God gives us a new spirit; we are no longer dead in sin, but alive through the power of the Holy Spirit. The old life is gone, and a new life has begun. Sadly, many people have never truly heard this before, even though they believe they are Christians.

When we share the Gospel honestly and simply, you can see people's eyes open. Something shifts. It's like they finally grasp what it truly means to be in Christ. That's what happened to these young men—and after praying with them—they knew they had received Christ before and were born again.

Religion Isn't Enough

Every believer should contemplate this question for themselves: "Have I truly been born again?"

My heart breaks for those who have not been discipled in the Word or taught about what a real relationship with God looks like. I can relate to them deeply and personally, as you know from my testimony in the beginning chapters of this book. I'd lie down at night and lack assurance of my salvation, hoping I was saved.

Many of the people we talk to are in the same place. They attend church, pray, and even get baptized—yet their hearts remain unchanged. Making Jesus Lord isn't just confessing the words; it's a heart decision to turn toward Him.

Jesus didn't come to improve our old lives—He came to make all things new. Without rebirth, there is no relationship—just religion.

Chapter Thirteen
Miracles, Signs, and Wonders

**"Through faith in the name of Jesus,
this man was healed—and you know how crippled
he was before. Faith in Jesus' name has healed him before
your very eyes."
(Acts 3:16 NLT)**

Do You Believe in Miracles?

A miracle is a supernatural act of God that interrupts the natural order to reveal His power, His presence, and His purpose.

Miracles point people to God's glory. When people witness miracles, their faith grows. Belief in God rises when something happens that cannot be explained—it has to be God!

In 2021, I discovered the teachings of many pastors and people of strong faith. Kevin Zadai was one of them. I was so gripped with his testimony and his teachings on healing—it was what my spirit had been seeking for so long. It awakened something within me. I listened to everything I could find. My faith began to grow in a way I had never experienced before. I *believed* God's Word so deeply that I wanted to live and operate in it. My mind was being transformed.

I bought two notebooks and began to write every word Kevin said —not because I was exalting his words, but because I wanted to stir up my own faith, renew my mind with God's truth, learn scriptures and how to apply it. I believed that if God could do it through him, He could do it through me.

I surrounded myself with several different translations of the Bible, Spirit-filled books, videos of teachings, and other training materials. With the Holy Spirit leading and guiding me, I began to teach myself.

Healing Testimony One: Leg Pain Lifted

One day, my sister, Kristy, called. Her friend was experiencing sudden, severe pain in her legs and could barely walk. She had ended up in the Emergency Room while out of town, but they couldn't help her. When she returned home, she asked my sister to call me for prayer.

Something shifted in me, instantly. My faith surged, and I knew in my spirit—she would be healed. I grabbed my anointing oil and headed over. On my way there, I cried as I sensed God's power already at work. I couldn't wait to see what He was going to do.

When we arrived, she hunched over, struggling to walk back to her chair. I could see how much pain she was in. I listened as she shared what she had been through over the past few days, and my heart broke for her.

I reminded her that Jesus had compassion, that He saw her, and that He wanted to heal her.

"He took the stripes on His back for your healing," I spoke. "I am a willing vessel—but I believe He will heal you. It is not me who heals; it's the Spirit of God in me. Will you believe with me?"

She said, "Yes."

I asked her permission to anoint her legs with oil. She agreed. I laid my hands on her calves and began to pray in Jesus' name, speaking healing scriptures over her. As I prayed, I felt her lower leg muscles moving. I thought she was flexing her calf muscles, but I didn't stop—I kept praying.

When I finished, I said, "Stand up and see how your legs feel." She stood slowly, looking around with a mix of wonder and disbelief.

"What does it feel like?" I asked.

"They don't hurt!" she said, looking over at her mom in amazement.

"Awesome! Take a step." I encouraged.

She began to walk—and then she walked around the dining table like nothing had ever happened!

My sister and I began to weep and praise the Lord! The power of Heaven filled that room. Her friend was laughing, smiling, and enjoying her healing.

Before I left, I asked, "Were you moving or flexing your calf muscles when I was praying?"

She looked at me, surprised, and said, "No, not at all."

That was God causing me to feel Him working. My faith increased even more. Wow, I almost lost it! God is so good!

On the way home, I praised God while listening to "Gratitude" by Brandon Lake, until I was so overwhelmed with emotion I had to pull over. When I got home, I continued to worship and cry tears of joy, lost in the greatness of God.

Healing Testimony Two: The Disappearing Mass

Another time, God performed a miracle through my hands. A woman had a growing mass about the size of an egg. When I laid my hands on her, I could feel it—solid, real. As I prayed, it suddenly deflated, as if the mass had been sucked out.

I told her to feel the area. She shouted, "You're not going to believe this. It's GONE!"

I said, "I know, I felt it leave!"

We praised God and jumped up and down, laughing and crying with joy.

Then she paused, "Wait," she said, "I still feel a little bit here."

"Okay," I said, "Let's get it all!"

I laid my hands over the area again. I could feel it too.

This time, it felt like a supernatural syringe removed it completely —just like the cysts I'd seen drained on an ultrasound back when I worked in mammography. Only this time, no needles required! Just the power of the Holy Spirit!

What are Signs and Wonders

A **sign** is a miraculous event that points to something greater. It confirms who God is, validates His Word, and reveals His power —like a signpost that says, "God is here."

"And the disciples went everywhere and preached, and the Lord worked through them, confirming what they said by many miraculous signs."
(Mark 16:20 NLT)

A **wonder** is an awe-inspiring act that leaves people amazed because it is clearly supernatural, far beyond anything human.

- A sign shows you where to look.

- A wonder makes you stop and look.

Think about Moses and the burning bush—he saw it and wondered—and then he moved toward it. He didn't walk away and wonder, "What was that?"

The Miracle Is Not Yours to Manufacture

Have I prayed for others who weren't healed in that moment? Yes. Have I wondered if I had enough faith or said the right words? Yes. Did I question if I should have said a different scripture or...a dozen other questions? Yes.

But here's what I've come to know: our healing is a benefit of the shed blood of Jesus—it has already been paid for.

The Scripture says:

"But He was wounded for our transgressions,
He was bruised for our iniquities;
The chastisement for our peace was upon Him,
And by His stripes we are healed."
(Isaiah 53:5 NKJV)

We might not witness instant miracles every time, but that doesn't mean healing hasn't started. Whether it happens supernaturally or gradually, God honors His Word.

His healing power isn't dependent on what we feel or see in the moment. We don't manufacture miracles—we simply walk in obedience and faith, making space for the Holy Spirit to do the work.

"And through the hands of the apostles many
signs and wonders were done among the people."
(Acts 5:12 NKJV)

God Is Still the God of Miracles

If you have never done it, I want to encourage you to step out in faith and pray for someone to receive a miracle. God is not looking for "super Christians"—there's no such thing. We are nothing without Him, but He's looking for willing vessels. People need healing everywhere we go. It's ok to be nervous—do it afraid, and your faith will rise.

God will build an unshakeable faith in you, but you must take the first step. Remember, the healing is not up to you—it's up to God when they get healed. If you are born again and desire God's will in your life, you are qualified. He is the one who qualifies you. He wants to operate through you and Jesus commands us to do so.

**"Go and announce to them
that the Kingdom of Heaven is near.
Heal the sick, raise the dead,
cure those with leprosy, and cast out demons.
Give as freely as you have received!"
(Matthew 10:7-8 NLT)**

God is still the God of miracles—healing, delivering, and revealing His power to those who believe. The same Spirit that raised Jesus lives in us and longs to work through anyone willing to say "yes."

You don't need perfect words. Just step out, trust Him, and watch your faith grow as He does what only He can do.

Be bold. Be willing. It's not about you—it's all about Him. It's about God's power flowing in and through you.

Chapter Fourteen

Empowered for More

"And everyone present was filled with the Holy Spirit and began speaking in other languages, as the Holy Spirit gave them this ability."
(Acts 2:4 NLT)

The Greatest Power of All

If you could choose any superpower, what would it be? We've all played that game, imagining flying over a city from a tall skyscraper, or walking through walls, or being in two places at once. But the greatest power of all isn't a fantasy—it's real. It's the power of the Holy Spirit, and much of the world knows nothing about it.

My heart in this chapter is to invite you into the "more" of God— the baptism of the Holy Spirit. Some may have never heard of this before, and that's why I want to open the door to a deeper understanding.

Salvation Is Just the Beginning

If you've placed your faith in Jesus, the Holy Spirit is alive in you. You are saved, forgiven, loved, and your name is written in the

Lamb's Book of Life. But did you know God has even *more* for you? The baptism of the Holy Spirit isn't a requirement—it's an invitation. It's not about salvation, it's about empowerment.

> **"And now you Gentiles have also heard the truth,**
> **The Good News that God saves you.**
> **And when you believed in Christ,**
> **he identified you as his own**
> **by giving you the Holy Spirit,**
> **whom he promised long ago."**
> **(Ephesians 1:13 NLT)**

> **"But you are not controlled by your sinful nature.**
> **You are controlled by the Spirit**
> **If you have the Spirit of God living in you.**
> **(And remember those who do not have the**
> **Spirit of Christ living in them do not**
> **belong to Him at all.)**
> **(Romans 8:9 NLT)**

The Spirit of God—the Holy Spirit—dwells in you the moment you believe.

Our Public Yes

On July 30, 2020, my husband and I were rebaptized in the Gulf of Mexico. What a beautiful experience! We were both baptized as young people, but this was our way of fully surrendering our lives to the Lord and publicly confirming our decision to follow Jesus wholeheartedly.

The Baptism of the Holy Spirit

This spiritual experience is a baptism that is different from water baptism. Any born-again believer in Christ can pray, lay hands on the sick, and see God move in miracles.

But this baptism equips believers who want more of the Holy Spirit to bring greater empowerment to walk in the gifts of the Spirit more freely, consistently, and with bold faith. This empowering gift is available to anyone who desires it. The baptism of the Holy Spirit isn't a requirement—it's an invitation. It's not about salvation, it's about power.

Jesus told the disciples not to even begin their ministry without it, because He knew how essential it was for their spiritual assignment, and we all have one.

**"Once when He was eating with them,
He commanded them, 'Do not leave Jerusalem until
the Father sends you the gift He promised,
as I told you before.
John baptized with water, but in just a few days you
will be baptized with the Holy Spirit."
(Acts 1:4-5 NLT)**

A Personal Encounter

On January 9, 2022, I received the baptism of the Holy Spirit, accompanied by evidence of speaking in tongues. I share this testimony because I want others to experience the fullness of Christ.

I once heard someone say, **"The baptism of the Holy Spirit isn't getting more of the Holy Spirit; it's letting the Holy Spirit get more of you."** That is precisely what it feels like.

Dunamis—is a Greek term meaning power and it is often used in Scripture to describe miraculous, Holy Spirit-empowered strength. It is heaven's power poured out into every believer. Speaking in tongues activates this power. We cannot afford to hold back. This is not the time for timidity, but for boldness in Christ. Dunamis power isn't given for comfort—it is given for impact.

> **"And everyone present was filled with the Holy Spirit and began speaking in other languages, as the Holy Spirit gave them this ability."**
> **(Acts 2:4 NLT)**

Everyone who was present in the Upper Room was already saved.

> **"I baptize with water those who repent of their sins and turn to God. But someone is coming soon who is far greater than I am—so much greater that I am not even worthy to be his slave and carry his sandals. He will baptize you with the Holy Spirit and with fire."**
> **(Matthew 3:11 NLT)**

> **"But you will receive power when the Holy Spirit comes upon you.**
> **And you will be my witnesses,**
> **telling people about me everywhere,**
> **in Jerusalem, throughout Judea, in Samaria,**
> **and to the ends of the earth."**
> **(Acts 1:8 NLT)**

Nothing Left on the Table

I don't want to leave anything on the table that God has for me while I'm here on this earth. We need everything He offers to fulfill His purpose and expand His Kingdom. The world is hurting, broken, and desperate for truth. The supernatural power of the Holy Spirit equips us to operate in wisdom, truth, miracles, and the gifts of the Holy Spirit.

If you desire to be baptized in the Holy Spirit, simply ask. You can pray privately, or you can ask your pastor or a trusted friend to pray with you. Like salvation, it is a gift you receive by faith. Seek Him. Ask to be filled and empowered. You won't regret it.

I have already prayed for you, and now you can join me in this prayer of agreement.

Heavenly Father,

I thank You for the person reading these words. I thank you for their hunger for more of You. I ask You to fill them with Your Spirit. Baptize them with Your power, Your love, and Your fire. Give them the evidence of Your Spirit by speaking in tongues—their own spirit language. Let them walk boldly in everything You have called them to. In your precious name, Jesus. Amen

The fire of God is still falling—for those bold enough to ask.

Chapter Fifteen
Finish Strong

**"I have fought the good fight, I have finished the race,
and I have remained faithful."
2 Timothy 4:7 NLT**

Called and Chosen

I hope by now you're not still wondering, "Can God really use me?" But if you are, I get you. As I have shared, I was a doubter and a cynic who struggled with believing I had a purpose given to me by God.

It's easy to feel unqualified or unsure of where to begin. But the truth is that if you're in Christ, you've been chosen to do good works for the Kingdom of God right here, on earth. You may not feel ready—and that's OK. Most people in the Bible weren't ready either, but all God needs is your "Yes."

The Power of a "Yes"

- Ruth's yes to God made her the great-grandmother of King David—part of Jesus' lineage.

- David's yes to God made him a giant slayer, opened the door to his destiny as king.

- Mary's yes to God made her the mother of our Lord and Savior, Jesus Christ.

- Peter's yes to Jesus turned a fisherman into a foundational apostle who helped launch the early church.

We can never know the power of our "yes" to God—until we say it. Maybe you are called to free a nation or a person from addiction. Perhaps you carry a gift of healing, and you see many people healed from sickness or disease. Perhaps you're called to lead a generation to freedom, and you will see Gen Z set the world ablaze with the fire of God.

You Were Made for Impact

Your "yes" is your legacy. One simple surrender to God plants a seed that He can multiply a hundredfold—because God is a multiplier. Imagine if the entire Body of Christ simply said, "Yes, Lord. Use me." Everyone has a part to fulfill. We're all on the same team–Team Jesus!

There's a saying I have heard, *"What can I do? I'm just one person— said seven billion people."* God planted a divine purpose inside you before the world ever began. You are not an accident.

Time is short. We are not promised one more day to make a difference. The world desperately needs Jesus!

Jesus said we would do even greater things than He did. That stirs something deep inside me. I want to rise up and fully step into the destiny God designed just for me. Every detail of His plan is written in heaven's books, and I don't want to miss a single part. His plans are not only good—they are perfect.

A few years ago, I dreamed I was running in a relay race. As the baton was passed to me, I realized I was the final runner. Whether it symbolized the final leg of my personal race or the last stretch of humanity's race, I felt urgency.

This is Our Moment

As the days grow darker, I do believe we are in the final chapter. Are we the chosen generation—young and old—who will finish the race. Signs and wonders are all around us, pointing to His soon return.

We are privileged to declare hope in the middle of chaos, shining God's light into the ever-growing darkness, and walking in the power of the risen Christ while the world asks, *"Why am I here?"* and *"Is God real?"* We have the honor and privilege of being disciples of Christ, sharing the Good News that changes lives forever!

The gospel will go to every nation; let this be the generation that carries it.

Kingdom Purpose Awaits

As you've read this book, has something stirred in your heart—an idea, a vision, or a deep sense that God is revealing something new to you? Could it be a revelation God wants to birth in you? If so, those seeds are being watered even now. He has created all of us for more than the routines, more than the mundane, more than going through the motions, more than the quiet life on the sidelines of faith, to step into Kingdom purpose.

God sees who you really are, and He is inviting you into *more* than you can imagine.

We are created for Kingdom impact, to reflect His glory, and to finish strong before we enter heaven's reward. God chose us to be alive for such a time as this, to help bring in the final harvest of souls who will live eternally with Him.

The legacy we leave behind isn't about success or wealth. It's about the "yes" we give to Jesus. When our lives are all said and done, without Jesus, what we leave are memories. But in Christ, we leave a foundation of faith that shapes generations to come. Our obedience sends ripples into eternity—waves that will one day testify to God's faithfulness long after we are gone.

The Final Harvest

We live in a remarkable time in history, marked by purpose and urgency. We have been chosen. This is our moment to prepare the way for Christ's return. The signs are everywhere, and I cannot stay silent. I cannot hide my faith and hope someone else will tell them. This is the hour. The harvest is ready.

So, let's throw off the fears and apprehensions. What can man do or say? God's perfect love drives out every bit of fear. Rest in Him. There is no striving in God's Kingdom. Armor up, because God is ready to partner with His people to populate heaven!

Through my journey, God has given me the privilege of leading people to Christ—something I do not take for granted. It all began with a straightforward question: "How can I pray for you?"

A life everlasting awaits the lost—but how will they know if we don't tell them?

We are called to lay hands on the sick, bring life to the dead, and preach the gospel to a lost and dying world.

We are part of the generation fulfilling this prophecy in Matthew 24:14 (NKJV):

> **"And this gospel of the kingdom will be preached in all the world as a witness to all nations, and then the end will come."**

How will we finish?

Let's finish strong!

> **"I don't mean to say that
> I have achieved these things
> or that I have already reached perfection.
> But I press on to possess that perfection
> for which Christ Jesus first possessed me.
> No, dear brothers, I have not achieved it,
> but I focus on this one thing:
> Forgetting the past and looking forward to what lies
> ahead, I press on to reach the end
> of the race and receive the heavenly prize
> for which God, through Christ Jesus, is calling us."
> (Philippians 3:12-14 NLT)**

Appendix
Created for More:
A Kingdom Guide to Sharing the Gospel

God has stirred something in you if you have made it this far. Maybe it's a fresh fire. Maybe it's a simple nudge that's been growing stronger. Maybe it's a desire to say, "Lord, you have my **'yes'** will you show me how?"

Whatever brought you here, this easy-to-follow guide will help you start sharing the gospel. It's not an in-depth training; it's a simple starting point, just enough to help you step out in faith, open your mouth, and trust God.

Whether you're stepping out for the first time or stepping out in a bolder way, the call is the same. **Go and make disciples.** You don't have to have all the answers; I sure don't. But Jesus does, and His Word does. You don't have to have attended a seminary, ministry school, taken hours of online classes, or read the entire Bible. All that is needed is a heart ready to love and serve God's people and allow the Holy Spirit to guide you, into the areas He has already designed just for you. He will gather the laborers. The harvest is ripe and waiting for us! Are you ready?

*It is important to note, some sources suggest it takes an average of seven times for someone to hear the Gospel before receiving Christ. As you explore the following ways to share, invite the Holy Spirit to familiarize you with each one so you can communicate the gospel effectively.

In this section, you will learn how to:

1. **Start conversations** at a prayer tent, on the street, event, festival, with friends, and with family.

2. **Share the Gospel** in your own words.

3. Share the message of salvation through the **Romans Road**.

4. Use the **Good Person** test to help people see their need for salvation.

5. **Respond with grace** to those who believe there is more than **one way** to heaven.

6. Use the **Bridge** analogy to show that the cross is the bridge to God.

7. Craft your **testimony**.

8. **Role Play** for Practice.

9. Use the **Next Steps** guide for new believers.

Start Conversations

Whether at a prayer tent or on the street, the goal is to carry a loving, warm, and welcoming invitation about you. It's all about love. Without love, nothing we do will have a lasting impact. So, engage with sincerity, kindness, and with the leading of the Holy Spirit.

Here are a few tips to effectively reach people and initiate conversations:

1. Before you head out, always start with prayer. Ask Holy Spirit to open your ears to hear, and give you His vision to see, and then proceed with the knowledge and trust that He will show you. Believe. Pray that God will bring people to the tent or highlight them if you are at a festival or mall. (i.e. *Highlight*—meaning to put an emphasis on someone or something you are drawn to.) Reach deep for God to lead you and show you. He will!

2. Keep your group small—ideally, two people, but no more than three.

3. Smile and greet them authentically and warmly. Smiles open doors. Eye contact shows people they matter. If possible, remove your sunglasses for better eye contact. Introduce yourself and ask questions like, "Are you from here or visiting?" You can offer little Jesus figurines as conversation starters. (There is a link to purchase from Amazon in the appendix.) Notice details like cross necklaces, tattoos, or pets as potential conversation openers.

4. Use these moments to strike up a conversation and build rapport. Be careful not to get too sidetracked; keep your focus on Jesus. Luke 12:12 (NLT) says, "For the Holy Spirit will teach you at the time what needs to be said."

5. Ask them if anyone has ever shared the Gospel with them. If they haven't heard the Gospel, consider one of the following methods to share it in your own words or through a short testimony.

The Gospel in Your Own Words

Here is a short summary of the Gospel in my own words. This is a framework, and it may never materialize in this form. The Gospel is the Good News of God's rescue plan for humanity. God's law could not save anyone from their sins or eternal separation from God. No one could keep the law, so God sent His Son, Jesus, to rescue us. He is the sacrificial Lamb of God, the only One who could fulfill the law because He had no sin.

> **"For this is how God loved the world: He gave His one and only Son, so that everyone who believes in Him will not perish but have eternal life."**
> **(John 3:16 NLT)**

Jesus lived the life we could not live. He was sinless and obedient. He died the death we deserved, taking the punishment for our sins. He rose from the dead, defeating sin, death, and the grave. Death could not keep Him.

> **"Christ died for our sins, just as the Scriptures said. He was buried, and he was raised from the dead on the third day, just as the Scriptures said."**
> **(1 Corinthians 15:3-4)**

Salvation is a gift we cannot earn. It is given to us by God's grace through our faith in Him. The Gospel is not about being good enough or working our way to heaven.

> **"God saved you by His grace when you believed. And you can't take credit for this; it is a gift from God. Salvation is not a reward for the good things we have done, so none of us can boast about it."**
> **(Ephesians 2:8-9 NLT)**

The Gospel isn't just about avoiding hell—it's about knowing God. It's a call to surrender our lives and follow Jesus as Lord and Savior. It's about repentance, relationship, and restoring the intimacy with God—through Jesus Christ—that was lost in the Garden of Eden with Adam.

**"Then He said to the crowd, "If any of you wants to be my follower, you must give up your own way, take up your cross and follow Me."
(Luke 9:23 NLT)**

The Romans Road

The Romans Road is a pathway to salvation using scriptures from the Book of Romans. It is one way to show the need for salvation.

Everyone needs salvation because we have all sinned. We are not perfect; therefore, we can't earn salvation. **"For everyone has sinned; we all fall short of God's glorious standard" (Romans 3:23 NLT).**

Jesus died for our Salvation. Even in our deepest sin, Jesus gave His deepest love—that even while in sin, He hung on the cross for us. **"But God showed His great love for us by sending Christ to die for us while we were still sinners" (Romans 5:8 NLT).**

Salvation is a Gift. A wage is a payment. The payment for sin is death. Jesus made our payment. **"For the wages of sin is death, but the free gift of God is eternal life through Christ Jesus our Lord" (Romans 6:23 NLT).**

Confess With Your Mouth. By confessing Jesus is Lord with your mouth, you declare He is not only Savior, but Lord over everything. **"If you openly declare that Jesus is Lord and believe in your heart that God raised Him from the dead, you will be saved." (Romans 10:9 NLT)**

Salvation Comes Through Faith. God justifies the sinner just as if they never sinned. It is faith and trust in Jesus that makes us righteous. **"But people are counted as righteous, not because of their work, but because of their faith in God who forgives sinners" (Romans 4:5 NLT)**

God Saves All Who Call to Him. If you call on the name of Jesus, you will be saved. **"Everyone who calls on the name of the LORD will be saved" (Romans 10:13 NLT)**

Continue asking questions to those you're speaking with to keep them engaged. Also, allow them time to process what they are hearing.

Questions are essential because they provoke people to think about the deeper things of God that they may have never considered before, such as:

"Have you ever heard this before?"

"What do you think about what I just shared?"

"Would you like to make a decision today?"

Never put pressure on anyone. You can usually tell if their heart has been softened by their countenance or tears. If they are not ready—no condemnation—just explain that asking Jesus to save them can be done anywhere, anytime. He is always waiting for a relationship with them. God meets each person in the middle of their real life. In the pain, the brokenness, and in the places, they feel most distant from God. He doesn't require perfection for their relationship. He just loves them. God will work out every detail; we just plant the seeds.

The Romans Road can be found by looking up the scriptures in the Bible, on your phone, by ordering tracks to distribute, or by memorizing it. There is even a Holy Bible that highlights the Romans Road, which is easy to use with thumbnail highlights when sharing the Gospel.

The Good Person Test

Many people believe they are going to heaven because they consider themselves to be good people. The belief that "works" like attending church, serving at church, participating in community service, raising a family, being faithful to one's spouse, working hard, praying, and reading the Bible are enough to get to heaven leads people astray. The Good Person test is a respectful way to show them their need for a Savior.

Maintain a tone that is kind, humble, caring, and compassionate. Be like Jesus, never force people, but reach them by loving them where they are.

Start a conversation: First, begin with an opening conversation. After that, go deeper and say, "We are out here talking with people about faith. Would you be willing to answer a few questions based on your life and the Ten Commandments?"

They may make this seem like a game or a lighthearted conversation, and that's OK. Go along with their response. Engage with them. Let them talk. Allow it to be easy.

Start with, "Do you think you're a pretty good person?" You will get a variety of answers on this one—some honest, some even funny—but it opens the door!

You could also ask, "Do you read the Bible?" or "Do you go to church?" These questions are merely warm-up questions to help you gauge if they know of God, so that you can see the direction of your conversation.

Next question, "I'm not going to judge you, but we will go deeper with questions, and you will judge yourself. Is that Okay?

"Have you ever told a lie, even a small one?" If yes, gently say, "We all have! What is someone who tells lies?" They will admit—A liar.

Next question, "Have you ever taken anything that didn't belong to you? What does that make you?"—A thief

Next question, "Have you ever used God's name as a curse word?" —That's called blasphemy, dishonoring God's name.

Next question, "Have you ever looked at a woman or man with lust in your eyes?—Jesus said if you look at someone with lust, you've already committed adultery. By your own admission, you've broken several commandments, just like I have.

Last question, "So, if God judged you today, would you be guilty or innocent?" Most people realize they are guilty.

Then say, "That's the bad news, but do you know what Jesus did for guilty sinners like you and me?" Most people can answer this, but if they don't know, say, "He died on the cross to pay our sin debt."

You can explain how we owed a debt based on the law, because no one could keep the laws (the commandments), so Jesus paid the debt, or the fine, with His blood—**PAID IN FULL.** Once a person realizes that they can't keep the laws and only Jesus can save them, they can receive salvation through faith. They may not be ready at that moment. You are planting seeds.

You can refer them to Living Waters (Ray Comfort) for more resources. www.livingwaters.com or Living Waters on YouTube.

How Can We Pray For You?

Another way to engage is to begin with an initial conversation and then say, "How can we pray for you?"

Then "Before we pray, I'd like to ask you a question: On a scale of 1-10, what is the likelihood of you going to Heaven?"

Most say any number other than 10.

You: "What do you believe would make that a 10?"

Response: "Well, I guess I should just try to do better and read my Bible more. I haven't read much lately, and I've been missing church."

You: "Can I tell you that salvation isn't based on performance or perfection?"

Good questions that get right to the point are, "Are you born again?" or "Have you ever heard the Gospel message?"

They may say they aren't sure, or they don't think so. Always ask by saying, "May I show you something in the Bible?" and then lead them down the Romans Road or ask them if you can share the Gospel in your own words.

Other options for questions you can ask are, "Do you believe that Jesus died, was buried, and rose again on the third day?" If they say yes, ask them, "Have you ever let Jesus guide every area of your life?" If they haven't, or they're unsure, you can invite them to do so.

It is more than knowledge to know that Jesus died; even the devil knows that. It is a heart that desires to be changed by God that saves them. Are they ready to believe, repent, and follow Jesus?

Let them know they can pray right then with you, or they can take that step at church or in private. The important thing is helping them understand that it's not just about believing in Jesus—it's about recognizing their need for a Savior, asking for forgiveness, and choosing to turn from sin (repentance). I like to explain it like this— that unrepentance (refusing to turn away from sin) can act like a dam in the heart, blocking the flow of God's love. But once the dam is opened through repentance, the heart becomes free and open, and God's love can pour in. Repentance is essential to salvation in Christ. Repentance is a change of the heart—a desire to turn from sin and to turn to Christ.

Which Way to Heaven

Do all roads lead to God? Many believe they do. The belief is that we love and accept everyone and everything, and as long as we are good and kind, and have good boundaries—we will get there—a little of this and a little of that, and we're good.

While engaging, you could ask them, "Can you tell me how to get to Heaven in the way you believe?"

> "**Jesus told him, "I am the Way, the Truth,
> and the Life. No one comes to the Father
> except through Me."
> John 14:6 (NLT)**

Jesus is not "a" way; He is "The Way." Point them to Jesus, with love and grace.

This scripture is clear and points directly to Jesus, not Buddhism, Judaism, Hinduism, Jehovah's Witnesses, or any other religion.

> **"Enter by the narrow gate; for wide is the gate and
> broad is the way that leads to destruction,
> and there are many who go in by it."
> (Matthew 7:13 NKJV)**

The narrow gate is by faith and obedience to God. The broad gate is the way for most people, the comfortable way, the way of deception and destruction.

To get to heaven, they must believe that we turn to God and receive new life from Him. **John 3:3 (NLT) says:**

> **"Jesus replied, 'I tell you the truth, unless you are born
> again, you cannot see the Kingdom of God.'"**

Tell them God loves them so much and His Word is true. Share the gospel if you can. Pray with them if possible. Give them a track. Bless them in any way you can.

The Bridge Illustration

Describe a visual of humanity separated from God by sin. The cross bridges the gap, allowing us to cross from death to life.

Imagine two cliffs. On one side stands humanity – you, me, and everyone. On the other cliff is God, holy and full of love for humanity. Between humanity and God is a huge separation—a canyon, gap, or chasm. The chasm is caused by sin, and we've all done it. We are all guilty.

**"For all have sinned and fall short
of the glory of God."
(Romans 3:23 NIV)**

No matter how hard we try, we cannot bridge the gap through good works or being a good person to get to God. But the Good news is, God does not want us separated from Him. So then, how do we get to God? He sent Jesus to bridge the gap between humanity and God. The cross bridges the gap, making a way for us to reconnect with God.

The cross made the way to cross from death to life. Such an analogy! People can get a vision for this and see it! I've used it and it works.

You can ask, "Did that resonate with you?" Or "Does what Jesus did make sense?"

You can place your faith in Him and receive salvation today, crossing the bridge to God. Jesus didn't point to the bridge; He became the bridge!

> **"I am the way, the truth, and the life. No one can come to the Father except through Me."**
> **John 14:6 (NLT)**

If you have a piece of paper, a napkin, and a pen, you can draw the picture above to help someone gain a deeper understanding. You can also create them on Canva or draw them, and then have a few printed for display.

Craft Your Testimony

When you're out praying for others and sharing the Gospel, one of the most powerful tools you have is your story—your personal testimony of what Jesus has done in your life. Your story doesn't have to be a dramatic transformation or full of scriptures—what matters are authenticity and clarity.

People aren't looking for a three-point sermon, but they will listen to a short story, especially 2-3 minutes. It's essential to keep it short. Attention spans are short—people have busy lives and don't have the time to listen to your whole life story, and honestly, they probably don't want to. But a quick story of "this is where I was and this is what God did for me," can change a life forever.

Here are a few questions to think about:

1. What was life before you knew Christ? What led you to Christ? Don't glorify sin—it's ok to reference the sin you were in, but don't magnify that. It's important to remember Christ is the focus.

2. How did you meet Christ? What was the turning point when you encountered God? Was it a prayer, a friend, a sermon, a concert, a dream?

3. What changed after Christ? Describe the person you have become. What difference has God made in your life? How is your life better because of Jesus?

Roll Play

Role-playing with our team has been a valuable tool in learning how to communicate clearly, share the Gospel, and navigate tough questions and challenges. This helps us as we respond with love and grace.

We challenge each other by creating scenarios. For instance, consider two people walking towards each other, with one stopping to engage in conversation, and let it roll from there. It's okay if we mess up because we are there to help each other, cheer each other on, and build confidence. We discuss ways to express ourselves more effectively.

Role-playing was an excellent practice for the festivals we attended. Festivals bring people from every culture, belief, and practice, as well as those with no belief or faith. You won't have all the answers, but when words fall short, just fall back on the truth: "Jesus loves you." Or "Be blessed." Or "How can we pray for you?"

Know your audience. If someone mocks or rejects you, don't fire back with "We'll be praying for you." Just walk away in love and kindness.

One thing I love about role-playing is the sense of unity it creates within the team. There's something powerful about stepping into boldness together—it builds camaraderie, trust, courage, and connection. You get to know one another on a deeper level, and before long, the fear of man starts to scatter like smoke in the wind. Bye-bye fear!

Next Steps

When someone accepts Christ, there is an atmosphere of love and the presence of heaven. Tell them they have made the most important decision of their life. The angels who have walked with them are celebrating—this is just the beginning. Hug them if you can. Rejoice with them. Tell them they are a child of God, and their name is written in the Lamb's Book of Life. Tell them to remember the date.

If they live in your area, invite them to your church and encourage them to connect with you. They need discipleship. The enemy just lost them and won't give up easily. If they don't live in the area, encourage them to attend a Bible-believing church, get baptized, and delve into God's Word.

If you have any tracks or materials, such as the Next Steps tracts (Link provided in the index) or the New Believer's Bible, please provide them. Encourage them to start with the book of John.

Resources are great but not required. What matters most is your **"yes"** and your heart for the lost. God will lead you. Don't let a lack of funds hold you back. As the saying goes, "If it's God's will, it's God's bill."

Salvation Prayer

Jesus, I believe You are the Son of God who died for my sins and rose again. I confess my need for You, and I ask You to forgive me. Come into my life, make me new, be my Savior and Lord. I give You my life—thank You for loving me, saving me, and showing me a new path with You. Amen.

Final thoughts

If you feel led to set up a Prayer Tent, all that is needed is a tent and two people with a heart for Jesus. If street ministry is your calling, all you need is two people. Don't stress over the handouts and go where the Spirit leads you.

If finances allow, consider ordering tools like:

- Scripture bracelets or Armor of God bracelets

- Gospel tracts

- New Believer Bibles or Booklets

- Simple signs or T-shirts that say, "Need prayer?" "Free Prayers" or "Need Hope?"

- Little Jesus figurines

Follow up by obtaining their phone numbers, inviting them to church, providing them with a church business card, and encouraging them to stay connected. Following Jesus is just the beginning; they don't have to do it alone.

God will use the smallest seed of obedience to produce eternal fruit. So go in boldness and love—and don't forget—**you were created for more in Christ Jesus.**

> **"Keep and live out the entire commandment that I'm commanding you today so that you'll live and prosper and enter and own the land that God promised to your ancestors. Remember every road that God led you on for 40 years in the wilderness, pushing you to your limits, testing you so that he would know what you were made of, whether you would keep his commandments or not. He put you through hard times. He made you hungry. Then he fed you with Manna, something neither you nor your parents knew anything about, so you would learn that men and women don't live by bread only, we live by every word that comes from God's mouth. Your clothes didn't wear out, and your feet didn't blister for 40 years. You learned deep in your heart that God disciplines you in the same way a father disciplines his child."**
> **(Deuteronomy 8:1-5 MSG)**

"Take delight in the Lord,
and He will give you your heart's desires."
(Psalm 37:4 NLT)

"But there's far more to life for us. We're citizens of
high Heaven! We're waiting for the arrival of the
Savior, the Master, Jesus Christ, who will transform
our earthly bodies into glorious bodies like His own."
(Philippians 3:20 MSG)

The End

A Letter to My Husband

My Joey—the love of my life:

Our journey together has been one of the greatest gifts of my life, and I love you more every day. You have loved me with such patience and kindness, cheered me on, and supported me through the seasons when all I could do was write, pray, and obey the quiet voice of God calling me deeper. You are my everything!

This book was born out of love and obedience to my Father—but I couldn't have written it without the love and steadiness of yours. You were one of the greatest ways God showed me His heart. Your kindness softened me in ways I didn't even realize I needed.

Before I fully surrendered to God, I believe He sent you to me—as if to say, "This is what my love feels like." And through your love, I started to believe that maybe I was worth being loved like that.

So, thank you for covering me when I needed courage, and for loving me—sacrificially, tenderly, and without conditions.

You are not just part of my story; you were the beginning of my healing journey. I love you with all my heart.

Always yours,

Caron

A Letter to my Children

To my beloved Shelby and Matt:

You are, and always will be, the greatest joy of my life.

As I wrote this book, my heart overflowed with love for both of you. This book holds stories of faith, surrender, and a journey I never expected—but through it all, you've been part of every step, woven into every prayer, and carried in every moment.

Several years ago, I followed a quiet pull toward the ocean—a longing I didn't fully understand at the time. I see now that it wasn't just the waves that were calling me; it was God. The voice of God was inviting me into something new—a touch that connects us all. He was leading me deeper, somewhere I could finally hear His voice in a way I couldn't before.

It wasn't about leaving; it was about being led. And while I may have moved miles away, please know this: not a single mile has ever lessened my love for you. You will always be a part of me.

My prayers cover you and your family daily. My heart carries you constantly, and my hope for your future is rooted in something eternal. God's plans for your lives are good—so much better than anything we could ever dream up on our own.

If you take nothing else from this book, let it be this: You are deeply loved. Not only by me, but by a God who sees you, knows you, has the best plan for your life, and has never taken His eyes off you.

With all my love, always,

Mom

Acknowledgements

God writes the story, but He fills the journey with people who help us rise, heal, and keep saying **"yes"** to God's call. We are never meant to walk our path alone—and I am forever grateful for the lives He has put in my life.

Missy Maxwell-Worton, you are one of a kind! Only God could have orchestrated our connection. I feel like I could laugh sometimes, because it's one of those stories I couldn't make up if I tried. Since the day you became my coach, mentor, and friend, you were a beacon of God's light in my life, continually speaking truth and calling forth creativity to write a redemptive book for Kingdom impact. Your wisdom, encouragement, and prophetic voice have fueled me to fulfill the promise God placed within me. What you have taught me is worth more than gold and is a direct result of listening to and obeying the Holy Spirit. I am so grateful for your **"yes"**!

Donna Bess, I am so blessed by you! I am so thankful for our friendship—the many laughs, the nights we have poured out to each other, powerful prayers, beach-time—and if all that wasn't enough, you're the best editor of my many "final" documents. Thank you for your patience, which allowed me to maintain my voice and convey the message I needed to share. You are a treasure. Thank you for all the work you put into this book and for making it very special. I am forever grateful and give thanks to God for placing you in my life at just the right time.

Thank you to all my Warrior Writer sisters—my tribe! What God has put together in our group is so rare and precious—like fine diamonds. The love, friendship, and deep connection we've shared as Warrior Writers is something I'll never forget. Growing together —being healed and equipped to write books of hope and transformation—will always be one of my most cherished memories.

Pastor Shawn Baker—I'm so grateful to the Lord for leading my husband and me to the church you shepherd. Being under this church's leadership encourages and equips me to walk more confidently in my calling for God's Kingdom. Your leadership helps shift my mindset—to be strong and courageous in the Lord, to trust His plans, and to step forward in greater faith. Thank you for your covering and the way you lead with purpose, intentionality, and the power of the Holy Spirit.

This book would never have been written had it not been for the obedience of Cody Boyett. You heard God's voice, and you relayed His message to me. I am genuinely grateful to you for unlocking a promise God had planned for me.

To my dear friend Bon Bon, I am so thankful to the Lord for you in my life. Though you aren't mentioned in this book, your friendship has shaped my life in countless ways as God has written my story. Sitting with you, praying for others, hearing you minister, and giving prophetic voice to so many—including over my own life —is one of the most meaningful parts of my journey. I am honored to sit under your wisdom and discernment, as well as your mercy and compassion for the hurting. You are a bright light in my life. Much love, Bon Bon!

A special thank you to Chris M. Smith and Tammy Largin for sharing your knowledge with the Warrior Writers on all things involving technology and design. From graphics and reels to book covers and business cards, from one-sheets to setting up a website– the giftings you share in areas like Canva, video, and social media have been an enormous blessing. I am not only thankful for our friendships, but also for the passion and creativity you pour into every detail of our training.

Thank you, Carolyn Searcy, for preparing and sharing your weekly inner healing classes with Warrior Writers. Your heart to help us heal our wounds—from childhood to adulthood, even the ones we didn't know were there—is a gift. That healing isn't just helping us;

it's making a generational impact—breaking chains! You are a blessing and a genuine friend.

I would like to extend a huge thank-you to all my beta readers! You are extra-special to me, taking the time out of your busy schedules to read my book, share feedback, and offer loving critique. Bon Bon, Cherie, Kristy, Paulina, Terri, and Tiffany, y'all are awesome!

Resources

The Good Person
www.livingwaters.com

Moments With the Book tracts
www.mwtb.org

Little Jesus figurines on Amazon
https://a.co/d/33KfGYA